NECESSARY ENDINGS

NECESSARY ENDINGS

THE EMPLOYEES, BUSINESSES, AND RELATIONSHIPS THAT ALL OF US HAVE TO GIVE UP IN ORDER TO MOVE FORWARD

Dr. Henry Cloud

HARPER
BUSINESS

An Imprint of HarperCollins*Publishers*
www.harpercollins.com

HarperCollins books may be purchased for educational, business, or sales promotional use. For information, please write: Special Markets Department, Harper-Collins Publishers, 10 East 53rd Street, New York, NY 10022.

FIRST EDITION

Designed by Renato Stanisic

Library of Congress Cataloging-in-Publication Data
  Cloud, Henry.
    Necessary Endings : the employees, businesses, and relationships that all of us have to give up in order to move forward / by Henry Cloud.—1st ed.
      p. cm.
    ISBN 978-0-06-177712-7 (hardback)
      1. Change (Psychology) 2. Organizational change. 3. Interpersonal relations. 4. Psychology, Industrial I. Title.
    BF637.C4C56 2010
    650'.13—dc22
                                    2010024369
10 11 12 13 14 OV/RRD 10 9 8 7 6 5 4 3 2 1

THIS BOOK IS DEDICATED TO THE LEADERS
WHO HAVE ALLOWED ME TO WALK WITH THEM
THROUGH THEIR NECESSARY ENDINGS.
YOUR COURAGE, CONVICTION, AND FAITH ARE INSPIRING.

Great is the art of the beginning, but greater is the art of ending.

—HENRY WADSWORTH LONGFELLOW

Contents

Preface

Today may be the enemy of your tomorrow.

In your business and perhaps your life, the tomorrow that you desire and envision may never come to pass if you do not end some things you are doing today. For some people, that is clear and easy to execute. They end the things that are holding them back. For others, it is more difficult. This book is about that problem and how to get the results you desire by ending the things whose time has passed.

In it you will see that endings are a natural part of the universe, and your life and business must face them, stagnate, or die. They are an inherent reality. You will also see that there are different kinds of endings and that learning how to tell one from the other will ensure some successes and prevent many failures and much misery, ending substantial pain and turmoil that you or your business may now be encountering.

You will learn that there are reasons why you may not see the endings that are right in front of you, and reasons why you have been unable to execute the ones that you do see but feel paralyzed to deal with. But more than learning to see them, you will also find successful strategies for dealing with them.

And you will find that there is hope for some people and some business problems that seem hopeless to you now, but the problem has been in misdiagnosing what there's hope for and where there's none, and in mistaking which tactics will not help realize that hope and which ones will.

All in all, *my* hope is that you will be comfortable and confident in seeing, negotiating, and even celebrating some endings that may be the door to a future even brighter than you could have imagined.

CHAPTER 1

Endings: The Good Cannot Begin Until the Bad Ends

There it was again, that sinking feeling in his gut. He was noticing it more and more, at the same time each morning. It was happening each time he pulled into his parking spot at corporate headquarters and turned the ignition off, in that moment of silence when the radio shut down and he hadn't yet opened his car door to go into the building. He could no longer deny that it was real nor that it had become consistent: he didn't want to go into the office.

He felt a heaviness inside that was the opposite of his natural drive. Stephen was the type who was always pushing ahead. As a kid, he was the first one to run onto the field; in a group, the one to say, "Let's go do this"; in a business crisis, the one to pick up the ball and move it forward, no matter what the obstacle. He was passionate by nature and had no problem engaging with life. But now, each morning in his car, he had to admit that he felt no strong drive to go into that building and gear up for another day of making it work. That drive had been replaced by this heaviness, which was anything but motivating. This was not a feeling that he was used to.

So on this particular morning he didn't do what he normally did, which was to reach into the well of his natural optimism and make himself dive in. Instead, he restarted his car and drove to a park he passed each day on the way to work. He spotted a bench that would do fine. He just wanted to think.

As he sat down, he realized two things. First, he had not really let himself do much of this: thinking. He had been too busy and caught up in the events of the last few years since he took the helm of the company, and he had not taken enough time to reflect. He had just worked *hard*, because it was needed. The company that he loved and had felt would be his home forever was not going where he thought it would go. It had stalled out more than a year ago, and it still wasn't turning around. Life seemed to be draining out of the business, and now it felt more like a task and a duty to run it than the love affair it had been in the beginning. The honeymoon was over, but he had treated that as just another challenge to immerse himself in. That was who he was.

But what he realized at this moment was that the activity level had kept him from thinking too deeply, and when he did allow himself to pause, he realized the second thing: if he did think deeply, he would run into some thoughts that he did not want to have.

But, on this morning, he allowed himself to go there. He asked himself questions: What is this heaviness inside really about? What is it that drains me?

When he got out of his own way and allowed himself to be honest with himself, it did not take long for his gut to speak to him.

First, there was the strategy of the whole thing. He had taken the CEO job because profits were good but not great. To him, that seemed like an opportunity. He was a performer, and throughout his career, he'd demonstrated that he truly could get more out of things than other people had gotten out of them before. He was smart, and he could execute. Using sheer horsepower and efficiency alone, he knew that there was growth in the existing numbers, not to mention in what new revenue he could realize through introducing new products and adding new sales territories.

But in the last year, with all of his talents and efforts applied as diligently as he knew how, the growth was not happening. That had to mean something else, and the something else was scary. It meant that the world was changing, the market was changing, but the company had not really changed with it. His team had just tried to do what they were already doing but do it better. And when he let himself realize the truth, he had to admit that the bright future he had imagined wasn't going to materialize until he made some big changes in direction.

To do that, though, would mean a lot of things to him that he didn't want to go through. It meant going to his board of directors and having a battle. It meant admitting that he had not been able to make the old way work, and to him that was admitting failure. Few things were worse.

But even worse than that, it meant some very hard decisions about people. A new direction that involved more technology and trickier financing would not work with many of the people he had in key positions. How would he remove them? Where would he put them? And even worse, would he have to get rid of them?

Related to that was one of the most difficult truths in this face-the-facts session. Although Stephen was the CEO, and "in charge," there was a crack in the foundation of his role that he had never fully addressed, and that was one of the biggest causes for his heavy gut: Chris. Chris was the son of the founder, put into his position of VP of Marketing by Stephen's predecessor, the founder's brother and Chris's uncle. Their hope at the time was that Chris would one day be the CEO, and they had placed him in this role as part of that succession plan.

But the truth was that not only was Chris not CEO material, he was not even the right stuff for an executive team. Stephen felt that he was carrying extra weight around with Chris in the way, and everything would be better if Chris were gone. To go there, however, would mean that he would be asking the company to make a huge choice: family or business? Every time he thought of that, he did not like either outcome. If he forced the question of Chris's future but lost, Stephen knew his plans for the future would be forever held back, and he would then be resented by the pro-Chris camp, not to mention by Chris himself. On the other hand, if the board allowed him to get rid of Chris, Stephen would be free of the obstacle but would live in the relational aftermath of it all. The cure might be worse than the disease.

But another part of him said that that is what real leaders have to do—make the hard decisions. When he thought about that, he took inventory. Could he deal with a complete overhaul, going to the board, and retooling the whole thing? Could he let go of people whom he truly cared about? And the big questions: Could he force the board to decide whether or not they would allow him to pick his own team? And if they said no, was he ready to leave and do something else where he wouldn't be shackled by an unsolvable problem?

As Stephen went through each of these questions, he felt two opposing emotions. The first was exhilaration, the kind of energy that he knew related to building a future that had life in it. The second emotion was fear, related to what would happen if he actually went through those doors to the future. But he also noticed something else: *the heaviness was gone*. It had been replaced with another feeling, a new kind of determination to face reality, which was simultaneously motivating and scary.

He knew that to cross that divide, to face the fear and jump over that canyon, would require doing some hard things, relationally and emotionally. And he also knew that crossing it was going to require him to learn some new skills, as he had never quite gone through a doorway as big as this one. But he also knew that in spite of all that, he could not keep going the way he was going. Stephen was ready to act, to give up on what wasn't working and to start focusing his attention on the changes that needed to be made. He got back in the car, started the engine, and headed back to the office—this time a little faster. He was ready. Nothing had changed in the business yet, but something had changed in Stephen.

What happened on that park bench and where he went from there is the subject of this book.

Stephen was at a moment that we all come to, or should come to, more regularly than we think. How we deal with those moments will determine much about the direction of not only our work but also our lives. Whether or not Stephen would follow through, what that follow-through would look like, and what it would require from him to do it and get to the future that either the company needs or he himself desires—all that is the subject of this book.

WITH FEW EXCEPTIONS, I always try to write about topics that pass three requirements: First, they must be issues that I have worked with extensively in real settings. This ensures that I am not writing about an idea, or a theory but real experiences, methods, and results. I want readers to feel that "this rings true" and is based in the real world where they live and work. I know no other way to have that happen than to do the work first, before I write about it.

Second, I prefer to write about topics that I see people connecting with in many settings as I work and speak. In other words, I may personally care about something but find that it is not a very big "felt need" for others. So the topics that qualify have to resonate with people where they are, in what they are going through, and for what they need. These topics, to me, have the most heat, because they help people identify and put into words things they are experiencing yet have never quite been able to understand and express. But when they see the issues made clear, something connects with them inside, and moments of insight and movement occur.

Third, the topics have to matter. I want to talk about issues and practices that have substantial leverage and, when implemented, can create quantum change. There are topics that are real and that people connect with but that are not monumental in their effect. Then there are those topics that have enormous impact, and those are the ones that pass the "this matters" test.

Which brings me to "necessary endings." It is a subject that results in immediate phone calls or e-mails after I talk about it. People say, "I got it . . . and I took a step that I now see I have been putting off for some time," or tell me they took some immediate actions as a result of the talk or the consultation. And the results can transform an individual or a company.

Necessary endings by their very nature are real and relevant and, when implemented, can bring incredible results. When needed endings are done well, people succeed. When they're done poorly or not at all, people don't. Let's take a look at why and how.

THE UNIVERSALITY OF ENDINGS
Why endings? Whether we like it or not, endings are a part of life. They are woven into the fabric of life itself, both when it goes well, and also when it doesn't. On the good side of life, for us to ever get to a new level, a new tomorrow, or the next step, *something* has to end. Life has seasons, stages, and phases. For there to be anything new, old things always have to end, and we have to let go of them. Infancy gives rise to toddlerhood, and must be forever shunned in order to get to the independence that allows a child to thrive. Later, childhood itself must be given up for people to become the adults that they were designed to be.

Getting to the next level always requires ending something, leaving it behind, and moving on. Growth itself demands that we move on. Without the ability to end things, people stay stuck, never becoming who they are meant to be, never accomplishing all that their talents and abilities should afford them.

In business, endings often are absolute necessities for a turnaround or for growth to occur. Businesses must sometimes let go of old product lines or even entire areas of business whose day has passed. To get to the next level and often even to sustain their companies' current levels of health, business leaders must shut down yesteryear's good ideas, strategies, or involvements in order to have the resources and focus to take their organizations to tomorrow. Sometimes it means that employees have to be let go too.

Endings are also an important factor in our personal lives. There are relationships that should go away, practices and phases that must be relinquished, and life stages that should come to an end to open up the space for the next one. A breakup, an ending of some friendships or activities, or an unplugging from some commitments often signals the beginning of a whole new life. It is a necessary step I refer to as pruning, a concept that we will examine in more depth in chapter 2.

Some endings are not a next natural step but are just as necessary. We wish they weren't, but they are. They come about not in pursuit of growth to the next level, but because something has gone wrong. It's been said that some things die and some things need to be killed.

Many times a business is stuck in something that is not working, and the leadership step required is to shut it down or pull out of it. It is failing and can't be fixed. Or there are poor performers who have been allowed to remain too long and need to be fired. On the flip side, some people should quit jobs that are causing them harm.

In the personal realm, we can get stuck in situations or relationships that are hurtful, problematic, or toxic and must be ended. Or sometimes it is not relationships we need to end but behaviors—destructive patterns and practices that hold us back. In many contexts, until we let go of what is not good, we will never find something that is good. The lesson: good cannot begin until bad ends.

In both normal life and life gone wrong, endings are a necessity. As the Byrds reminded us in their Sixties song "Turn, Turn, Turn," there is a season to everything. Taken from Ecclesiastes, the message is that there is a season for things to begin and a season for them to end, and that's how life works. Perhaps you have heard or read this famous passage many times, but take another look and focus your attention on the prevalent role of endings throughout:

> *There is a time for everything, and a season for every activity under heaven: a time to be born and a time to die, a time to plant and a time to uproot, a time to kill and a time to heal, a time to tear down and a time to build, a time to weep and a time to laugh, a time to mourn and a time to dance, a time to scatter stones and a time to gather them, a time to embrace and a time to refrain from embracing, a time to search and a time to give up, a time to keep and a time to throw away, a time to tear and a time to mend, a time to be silent and a time to speak, a time to love and a time to hate, a time for war and a time for peace.*

Endings are not only part of life; they are a requirement for living and thriving, professionally and personally. Being alive requires that we sometimes kill off things in which we were once invested, uproot what we previously nurtured, and tear down what we built for an earlier time. Refraining, giving up, throwing away, tearing down, hating what we once cherished—all are necessary. Endings are the reason you are not married to your prom date nor still working in your first job. But without the ability to do endings well, we flounder, stay stuck, and fail to reach our goals and dreams. Or worse, we remain in painful and sometimes destructive situations. Endings are crucial, but we rarely like them. Hence the problem.

WHY WE AVOID ENDINGS

Endings are necessary, but the truth is that we often do not do them well. Although we need them for good results to happen in life and for bad situations to be resolved, the reality is that most of us humans often avoid them or botch them.

- We hang on too long when we should end something now.
- We do not know if an ending is actually necessary, or if "it" or "he" is fixable.
- We are afraid of the unknown.
- We fear confrontation.
- We are afraid of hurting someone.
- We are afraid of letting go and the sadness associated with an ending.
- We do not possess the skills to execute the ending.
- We do not even know the right words to use.
- We have had too many and too painful endings in our personal history, so we avoid another one.
- When they are forced upon us, we do not know how to process them, and we sink or flounder.
- We do not learn from them, so we repeat the same mistakes over and over.

Question: As you reflect on these reasons, can you think of any situations where these reasons have interfered with an ending you needed to make?

The aftermath of the global economic crisis of 2008 has required significant and largely unanticipated "resets" in major companies, forcing many to initiate painful and significant restructuring. At the same time, the crisis also brought to a head many problems that had long been apparent yet were never acted upon. *There were endings waiting to be had, needing to be had, yet unexecuted.* Why does that happen?

The American auto industry, for example, was forced to finally discontinue brands that cost more to manufacture than they produced in profits.. Certainly some accountant had done the math, but the necessary endings still weren't executed until the crisis or bankruptcy courts forced the issue. Why?

Many other kinds of businesses stepped up and cut fat out of their bureaucracies, only to realize later that the cuts had been long overdue. The economic crisis gave them the push they needed to do what they should have done much sooner. In the months following the meltdown, many leaders told me things like this: "Some of this crisis was good for us. These are changes we should have made years ago."

The leadership growth question then became, "Why didn't you?" Figure that out and you won't wait next time. Likewise, more than a few leaders also told me that they were grateful the crisis gave them the excuse to remove staff members who stood in the way and kept the company from going where it needed to go. Again the question is, "Why were those people still there?"

THE REAL REASON
The answers to the "why" questions typically have little to do with the business itself. Often, there are no good business reasons for waiting to do something that should be done now. Of course, there are times when potential collateral damage to other aspects of the business or other strategic issues makes it prudent not to execute an ending, but that is the exception not the rule. The real reason is this:

Something about the leaders' personal makeup gets in their way.

Leaders are people, and people have issues that get in the way of the best-made ideas, plans, and realities. And when it comes to endings, there is no shortage of issues that keep people stuck.

Somewhere along the line, we have not been equipped with the discernment, courage, and skills needed to initiate, follow through, and complete these necessary endings. We are not prepared to go where we need to go. So we do not clearly see the need to end something, or we maintain false hope, or we just are not able to *do it*. As a result, we stay stuck in what should now be in our past. And these abilities are not only lacking in the world of business. They appear in the personal side of life as well.

Think of the now ubiquitous "failure to launch" syndrome of those twenty- or thirty-somethings still living with their parents. They cannot end childhood and fully enter adulthood. But the bigger issue is often the parents' inability to end the pattern and stop the toxic dependency by pushing the grown "kid" out of the nest. They refuse to end their "helping" role, which is not in fact helping. Another tragic example is the inability of many women to walk out the door when they are being abused. Fears and vulnerabilities keep them stuck in devastating patterns that ought to end. Likewise, in the world of work, because of security fears, some cannot leave jobs that are keeping them stuck and unfulfilled. In sum, we are not prepared or equipped to take the next step, the one we really need to take.

And it is not only the endings that we must proactively execute that are problematic. There are also the endings that are forced upon us, endings we do not choose but that we cannot work through very well either. As a result, we remain in pain or stuck, unable to pursue a new phase in life. These endings include divorce, being fired or laid off, death of a loved one, disintegration of a friendship, chronic illness, and so on. We do not choose these endings; they are thrust upon us by people we have trusted or sometimes by truly horrible events in life. If we are not prepared or have had too many losses before, these endings can render us broken, depressed, and floundering, sometimes for years.

When we fail to end things well, *we are destined to repeat the mistakes that keep us from moving on.* We choose the same kind of dysfunctional person or demoralizing job again. Not learning our lessons and proactively dealing with them, we make the same business or personal mistakes over and over. Learning how to do an ending well and how to metabolize the experience allows us to move beyond patterns of behavior that may have tripped us up in the past. We do not have to keep repeating the same patterns.

Necessary Endings will address these issues in ways that will improve your business and personal life. It is my goal to share with you principles and practices that you can put into immediate action to:

- Help you become aware of the absolute necessity for some endings to occur in your business or your life;
- Equip you to diagnose when a business or a relationship has hope of getting better and when it should end;
- Equip you to diagnose what kinds of people deserve your trust and those who don't;
- Bring *endings* into the common language of your workplace so that pruning and continuous improvement become part of the culture;
- Normalize the idea of endings, so you can expect them instead of being surprised by them, and so you're able to deal with them as a normal part of what you do;

- Help you to actually get comfortable with endings;
- Help you understand why you have not been able to nego-tiate previous endings successfully;
- Show you how to execute endings well;
- Create vision and energy for a better future as you become unstuck; and
- Help you to stop repeating the same issues over and over again.

Endings are a part of every aspect of life. When done well, the seasons of life are negotiated, and the proper endings lead to the end of pain, greater growth, personal and business goals reached, and better lives. Endings bring hope.

When done poorly, bad outcomes happen, good opportunities are lost, and misery either remains or is repeated. So let's get em-powered to choose the necessary endings, execute them well, and get to the better results we all desire.

CHAPTER 2

Pruning: Growth Depends on Getting Rid of the Unwanted or the Superfluous

I am not very good at growing plants. Somehow the gardener's microchip did not get implanted when I was at the factory. But I have always had great admiration for those who are good at growing things. Especially roses. If you have ever seen a healthy rosebush with its vibrant, fully mature blooms, you know the admiration that the one who nurtured that beauty deserves. So how do these people do it? Certainly there is talent and art behind every beautiful garden. But there is also a method behind the beauty. It is called *pruning*. Pruning is a process of proactive endings. It turns out that a rosebush, like many other plants, cannot reach its full potential without a very systematic process of pruning. The gardener intentionally and purposefully cuts off branches and buds that fall into any of three categories:

1. Healthy buds or branches that are not the best ones,
2. Sick branches that are not going to get well, and

3. Dead branches that are taking up space needed for the healthy ones to thrive.

Necessary Ending Type 1

Rosebushes and other plants produce more buds than the plant can sustain. The plant has enough life and resources to feed and nurture only so many buds to their full potential; it can't bring all of them to full bloom. In order for the bush to thrive, a certain number of buds have to go. The caretaker constantly examines the bush to see which buds are worthy of the plant's limited fuel and support and cuts the others away. He prunes them. Takes them away, never to return. He ends their role in the life of the bush and puts an end to the bush's having to divert resources to them.

In doing so, the gardener frees those needed resources so the plant can redirect them to the buds with the greatest potential to become mature roses. Those buds get the best that the bush has to offer, and they thrive and grow to fullness. But the rosebush could not do this without pruning. It is a necessity of life for rosebushes. Without the endings, you don't get the best roses. That's necessary ending type 1.

Necessary Ending Type 2

Some branches are sick or diseased and are not ever going to make it. For a while, the gardener may monitor them, fertilize and nurture them, or otherwise try to make them healthy. *But at some point, he realizes that more water, more fertilizer, or more care is just not going to help.* For whatever reason, they are not going to recover and become what he needs them to be to create the final picture of beauty he wants for the bush and the garden. These are next to go: necessary ending type 2.

As a result, the bush now has even *more* fuel and life to pour into the healthy buds. The plant is now fully on mission, focusing its energy every day on feeding and growing the buds that are destined to reach full bloom and maturity.

Necessary Ending Type 3

Then there are the branches and buds that are dead and taking up space. The healthy branches need that room to reach their full length and height, but they cannot spread when dead branches force them to bend and turn corners; they should be growing straight for the goal. To give the healthy blooms and branches room and an unobstructed path to grow, the dead ones are cut away. This is an example of necessary ending type 3.

Pruning enables rosebushes and other plants to realize full potential. Without it, they are just average at best and far less than they were designed to be. If you think about it, there should never be an average rosebush. By nature, there is nothing average about them at all. They are designed for incredible beauty and lushness. But if not adequately pruned, they never make it. And like rosebushes, your business and your life also need the same three types of pruning to be all that you desire.

PRUNING YOUR BUSINESS AND YOUR LIFE

Do a dictionary search on *pruning* and you'll discover phrases like this:

A function of cutting away to reduce the extent or reach of something by taking away unwanted or superfluous parts.

Wow, if only we would lead and live by definitions! In the simple word *pruning* is the central theme of what a necessary ending is all about:

*Removing whatever it is in our business or life whose reach
is unwanted or superfluous.*

In business and in life, executing the three types of necessary endings described above is what characterizes people who get results. (1) If an initiative is siphoning off resources that could go to something with more promise, it is pruned. (2) If an endeavor is sick and is not going to get well, it is pruned. (3) If it's clear that something is already dead, it is pruned. This is the threefold formula for doing well in almost every arena of life.

The areas of your business and life that require your limited resources—your time, energy, talent, emotions, money—but are not achieving the vision you have for them should be pruned. Just like an unpruned rosebush, your endeavors will be merely average without pruning. And here is the key point: by average, I don't mean on an absolute basis. There is nothing wrong with being in the middle of the bell curve in many aspects of life, as that may be what success is for that person or at least that dimension of life. I have friends who own small businesses of less than average size in their industry or by other measurements, yet they have a fully maximized, thriving enterprise for what it is and is supposed to be. Hundreds of employees and tens of millions of dollars is a great rose of a business and a life for what their talents, dreams, and opportunities consist of. Not the size of Microsoft perhaps, but they have achieved *fullness of maturity for their company and/or life. Alive and thriving to the max. But without pruning, they would not have gotten there.* And by the same token, if Microsoft or a much bigger company with tens of billions in revenues is *not* pruning, just because they are large, they can still be "average" relative to their own potential. They can truly be lagging behind where they should be.

So the question is more about this: are you only achieving average results in relation to *where you or your business or team is supposed to be*? In other words, given your abilities, resources, opportunities, etc., are you reaching your full potential, or are you drifting toward a middle that is lower than where you should be if you were getting the most from who you are and what you have? When pruning is not happening, average or worse will occur.

Too often, as bad as the results of not pruning can be, we still persist in avoiding it because it involves fear, pain, and conflict. Yet in order to succeed, we *must* prune. How does that make you feel? Conflicted? Welcome to the inner turmoil of necessary endings.

GUT CHECK

In upcoming chapters, we will look at what lies behind our tendency to avoid pruning and how to name and resolve those issues. But before we get to the specifics, I want to ask you to ask yourself a few questions. Really ask. And if you are doing this with your team, ask these questions together:

- **What is your intellectual response to the idea of pruning?** Do you affirm or question the three kinds of pruning described above (too many buds, sick buds that will never recover, dead buds taking up space)? If you are on a team, are you all in the same place on the issue? If not, where is the misalignment? Ask around the table.
- **What is your emotional response to the idea of pruning?** Does it turn your stomach? Does it feel mean or uncaring when people are involved? Does it make you anxious in some way? Is it energizing? All of the above? If you are on a team, how do your emotional responses differ? Ask around the table.

It's vital to consider these questions because everything that follows is built on the premise that pruning is necessary, natural, and beneficial for anything that is alive. We need it developmentally (as we saw in chapter 1), and we need it in relationships and in business. We need it when things are going well and when things are not going well; it is a natural part of life's seasons and a requirement for growth.

If we accept the premise that pruning is necessary but still notice that we have an emotional misalignment with that premise, we will struggle to realize our vision of the future and our potential. But if you can become aware of your resistances and internal conflicts now, then you can begin to face them and work them through. If you have an intellectual antipathy to the concept of pruning, then I ask that you acknowledge that and agree to withhold judgment until you have read further.

Write down your answers to those questions. We will revisit them later when we look at the specifics of how our resistance to endings works. Suffice it to say at this point, though, that we all have them, and becoming aware of them and facing them is an important step to getting where you want to go.

Here is a recent example I encountered in a coaching session with Ellen, a high-level executive in a multibillion-dollar company. She had recently earned a significant promotion that moved her from the ranks of management into a senior leadership position. As a result, she was now responsible for creating the organizational strategy she had previously just implemented. Ellen knew she faced some challenges in making the transition.

"If I am going to make this work, if we are going to get from here to there, some people who have had leader roles are going to have to be moved out, because they are just not leaders. And in the new structure we really need true leaders. We won't reach our goals if we don't make that change," she said.

"Yes, and that will be your role. So where are you out of alignment with that?" I asked.

"Finding out that they don't have leadership roles in the new structure will be devastating to many of them," she said. "For my entire career, I have had a practice . . . I always think about the people I manage and see them in their cars driving home from work. I picture the kind of mood they are in and want them to be up and enthusiastic about their day at the company, and I work hard to make those rides home as positive as I can. But if I do what is needed, there are going to be some very negative rides home. I hit a wall when I think about it. It's like it makes me go in two different directions inside," she explained.

"Sounds like you think that 'negative' is bad," I reflected.

"Well, of course it is. I would not want them having that kind of day," she said.

"Have you ever had an infected tooth pulled?" I asked.

"Sure."

"Did you have a nice ride home?" I asked.

(*Laughing*) "No, it was awful."

"Well, that was negative, . . . or was it?" I asked. "If you define *negative* as feeling crummy, I agree it was. But if you define *negative* as 'harmful,' I would not call it negative but positive. It was not harmful at all for the dentist to inflict that pain. In fact, it was a very positive event, right? A healing event?" I asked.

"Yes, sure it was," she said.

"There is a big difference between *hurt* and *harm*," I said. "We all hurt sometimes in facing hard truths, but it makes us grow. It can be the source of huge growth. That is not harmful. Harm is when you damage someone. Facing reality is usually not a damaging experience, even though it can hurt."

I could see by Ellen's expression that the implications of what I was saying were starting to sink in. "*As a leader, you have got to re-*

define what positive and negative is. Positive is doing what is best and right for the business and for the people. And nearly always, letting someone know that they are not right for a position is one of the biggest favors that you can do for them. There are only three possible results of doing that, and two of them are good. The other is good also, in that if it happens, you for sure had the wrong kind of person in the job," I said.

"What are they?" she asked.

"First, if they find out that they were not performing, they may get better at their performance and turn into someone who can achieve. Your intervention helped them face the reality about themselves and moved them further along. If you had not done it, their next boss would have had to do it, and they would have lost another year or five. And go through all of that pain again. So you helped them face the truth about themselves and get better.

"Second, it may be that they are just miscast. And they need to find that out. Many, many times, when someone is removed, it is not because they are not talented but because they are in the wrong job or even business. The removal makes them face that; they find themselves, and they have a great next forty years. You helped them get off a road of failure and onto one of success. That is another great favor you are doing them.

"The third possible result—and the one that is diagnostic—is that they do not see that they need to improve or that they are trying to do something they are not cut out for, and they blame you or the company for their failure and go away bitter. They cannot see the truth and use it. They hate you and see themselves as a victim of your leadership. If that happens, you find out that you had someone in a key position who was probably not a learner (we will talk about diagnosing people later), and you have protected the company and yourself from their effects going forward.

"It is sad but true that some people just cannot face the truth when it causes them discomfort, *but that cannot be a reason that guides your decisions.* So in that case, you are lucky to find it out and be done with that person's lack of performance, but moreover, done with their entrenched attitude about feedback," I said. "And remember, the big result of all of this is that you have moved the company and yourself toward the vision becoming a reality. That is your big responsibility."

"Wow," she said. "I have never thought that causing hurt for someone could be a positive thing. That could make it *a lot* easier to execute."

Certainly, as we went on to discuss, the goal is not to cause pain for people. But sometimes reality does just that. Reality sometimes makes us face things that hurt, and that can be a very good thing. For her, this conversation was a paradigm shifter that was going to enable her to do some "conflict-free" pruning, a concept we will hear more about later.

WHAT IS THE PURPOSE YOU'RE PRUNING TOWARD?

When we talk about necessary endings, it's one thing to understand the theory behind the three reasons for pruning—good but not best, sick but not getting well, and long since dead—but it's another thing entirely to apply those concepts in real life. We can't execute endings in theory only, so they have to be clear in reality. The question is, What defines reality?

When pruning a rosebush, the first step is to ask, "What does a rose look like?" In other words, you have to know the standard you are *pruning toward.* The gardener knows what a healthy bud, branch, or bloom looks like and prunes with that standard in mind. The same thing is true in business and life—we have to have a good definition of what we want the outcome to look like and prune toward that.

For Ellen, the growth goal that the company had was the standard. The vision set by the CEO was crystal clear. That was why being put into her new position with his vision had so well defined what she had to do and made the conflict come to the surface for her. It *forced the pruning moment*. The pruning moment is that clarity of enlightenment when we become responsible for making the decision to either own the vision or not. If we own it, we have to prune. If we don't, we have decided to own the other vision, the one we called average. It is a moment of truth that we encounter almost every day in many, many decisions. For Ellen, the CEO's mandate had forced the pruning moment. She knew that if she shied away, as her initial internal conflict inclined her to do, she would fail to own the vision.

So step one for yourself or your business is naming the "rose"—in other words, defining the standard or goal you're pruning toward. There is no one right answer, but without some clarity on what you are trying to achieve, you won't know where to begin to bring about the necessary endings.

One of my favorite examples of this is the story of Jack Welch at GE. Welch was one of the best-known pruners in the annals of business. His approach illustrated both the success that pruning can engender as well as the conflict that it inherently brings to the surface.

Welch used four standards to make pruning decisions. Under his leadership, GE grew from $26 billion in revenues to $130 billion and from around $14 billion in market value to over $410 billion, making it the most valuable company in the world at the time. Here are the four standards Welch used to answer the question What are we pruning toward?

1. If a GE business could not be number one or number two in its market, it would be cut.

2. Any business that was struggling (sick) would be "fixed, closed, or sold."
3. Every year, GE would fire the bottom 10 percent of the work force.
4. Welch would get rid of the layers of bureaucracy in the company that slowed down communication, productivity, and ideas.

These criteria paint a crystal-clear picture of what GE was pruning toward. And as you can see, it is not without the inherent conflict that pruning naturally brings to the surface. On the one side, GE's success was undeniable. Besides the growth and valuation results mentioned above, it led to a time when twelve out of GE's fourteen business units were leading their markets. On the other side, it earned Welch the nickname Neutron Jack, as over a hundred thousand people were laid off during his tenure. The principle of firing the bottom 10 percent had a negative image in a lot of people's minds.

Welch's standards illustrate many components of pruning. Being number one or two in the market clearly demonstrates the reward of clipping some of the buds that are alive and growing *but are not the ones that will make it to the top.* Remember, I said that a bush is going to produce more buds than it can sustain, and the gardener has to decide on some basis which ones will remain and get to draw nourishment from the stalk. For GE, being first or second is that concept in action. *It is in complete alignment with the reality that both businesses and individuals will begin, gather, and have more activities than they can reasonably sustain.* Some of those activities may be good, but they are taking up resources that your best ones need. So you always will have to choose between good and best. This is especially tough for some creative people, causing them a lack of focus. They create more than they can focus on and feed, they are attached to every idea as if they were all equal, and they try to keep them all alive. Instead of a to-do list, they have a to-do *pile*. It goes nowhere fast.

Welch's "fix, close, or sell" standard addresses type 2 necessary endings: There will always be sickness. Businesses and people have issues. Our responsibility is always to "embrace the negative reality," as I have written about before in my book *Integrity*. And the *way* we address it should also give us a good diagnosis as to whether or not a problem or a person can be fixed. We will see that in the diagnostic sections later in the book, but the point now is that *we should not be dealing with negative realities in the same old way, over and over again*. At some moment, we have to determine whether or not our efforts to make a business succeed or to make a person improve are going to work. To do the same thing over and over again expecting different results is not only crazy, it is a recipe for staying stuck and not getting the rose you want.

Your attempts to fix should also include a realistic assessment of the potential for recovery and whether or not you are indulging in false hope. Leaders by nature are often optimistic and hopeful, but if you do not have some criteria by which you distinguish legitimate optimism from false hope, you will not get the benefits of pruning. *Sometimes, the best thing a leader or anyone else can do is to give up hope in what they are currently trying.* As we read in Ecclesiastes, there is a time to give up. Wise people know when to quit. Winners don't throw good money after bad. Or as the song says, they "know when to hold 'em, know when to fold 'em." Welch's phrase to "fix, close, or sell" clearly implies that there will be diagnostic criteria that will force a pruning moment. Some people have a mantra of "fix, fix, or fix," but they never do because that branch or bud or person is just not going to be fixed, period. It's time to move on.

The "fire the bottom 10 percent" mantra is a clear pruning idea that encompasses all three categories—good but not best, sick and not getting well, and long since dead. I am sure that in GE's bottom

10 percent there were some good ones, some not-getting-well ones, and some who were just not producing at all, the deadwood. And I can understand why many people were upset with a fixed strategy like that for firing employees. But I do believe that there is *some number* of people in every organization and every life who will be routinely "let go" if leadership is doing its stewardship job. The very nature of people is that there are some good ones who are not right for you, some sick ones in denial who are not going to change, and some who are adding nothing. *Always.* So if no one ever leaves your organization or your life, then you are in some sort of denial and enabling some really sick stuff all over the place. And it probably is accumulating. I have found this to be rampant in companies that have a high "people value." The value is good, but sometimes it keeps them from doing what is truly valuing to people.

So, was Welch really a Neutron? I will leave that for you to decide. My point is not that you have to have a strategy of firing a certain number or percentage; my point is that if you are truly leading, you *will* be firing *some* percentage. It is almost a truism. If you are not firing someone at some time, something is probably wrong.

Welch's intolerance of bureaucracy illustrates well the pruning concept that there are some branches that are just in the way. They are not adding anything, and they are definitely in the way of the growth of the other buds. In Welch's thinking, the bureaucratic layers kept the bright ideas and practices of workers from growing and being implemented into the structure of the company. Welch got the branches out of the way, and the growth propelled the company upward.

Good but not best, sick and not getting well, and deadwood taking up space. All three can be seen in these mantras that have been heralded to account in large part for the growth that GE experienced.

In this story, both the success and the conflict of pruning are so apparent. Pruning is not easy. It is hard and there will be people who don't like it, no matter what you do. You have to decide where your lines are, the values with which you will execute them, and go forward. Whether or not you prune in the Welch way is not the point, as his way doesn't fit all businesses or lives. The point is that no matter what your goals, vision, values, and metrics may be, they will force you to the pruning moment when you use them as the standards to evaluate situations and people.

Not every activity nor every person is a rose or will ever be one. One might be a great chrysanthemum, but remember, you are growing a rose of a business or life. So you have to begin by defining what you are pruning toward and the criteria by which you will keep or clip. We will spend time later helping you diagnose when to keep, fix, or clip, but for now what I want to emphasize is that step one has to be figuring out who you are and who you want to be. Two questions apply: How will you define success? and How will you measure it?

You can't prune toward anything if you don't know what you want. You have to figure out what you are trying to be or build and then define what the pruning standards are going to be. That definition and those standards will bring you to the pruning moments, wherein you either own the vision or you don't.

I recently had a coaching project with a venture capital group in the process of selecting an executive team for a new business launch. With the CEO now in place, they were evaluating candidates for the rest of his senior team. Using a five-point rating scale, with five being the best, I spent the day with them as they reviewed candidates. There were some very good people, but when I stepped back a bit, I noticed something peculiar. The individual candidates' performances were rated as mostly threes and sometimes fours. Because they were rating them individually, they were missing the bigger picture. I told them that if they chose all of these people, they would ensure that the new company would have level 3 returns. Is that the kind of returns they had promised their venture fund? Probably not. The conversation turned at that point to getting a better definition of what a rose was and how to measure it.

"If you don't know where you are heading, you'll get there" applies to pruning as well. Define what you are shooting for, and then prune against that standard. That is when vision, goals, and even teams begin to take the shape that you desire.

MORE THAN CUTTING EXPENSES

Sometimes people equate the concept of pruning with cutting expenses or "reducing head count." They say things like, "You're right. We have got some fat around here and need to cut some costs." But cutting costs is not what pruning is about, and when someone says that, they are thinking more like a manager than a leader.

Certainly, routine expense reviews and cuts are good pruning practices, always. They should be done, and we should consistently ask ourselves, *Do we really need to be spending that?* (And have you noticed that many times after expense cuts the businesses are doing just as well?) That's a good pruning exercise, but it misses the bigger picture.

The kind of pruning I'm talking about has to do with *focus, mission, purpose, structure, and strategic execution.* A mere expense cut might have enabled GE to keep all of the two hundred or so businesses it got rid of, if it had just followed a mantra to cut all expenses by 10 percent. As a result, the "average roses" would have then become even less than average, and we would not still be talking about GE's accomplishments. So what we are talking about here is not just "cutting fat," as the phrase goes. We are talking about defining what the bush is going to look like and pruning everything that is keeping it from realizing that vision—be it good, bad, or dead. And that vision could be business or personal in nature.

In many businesses and in many people's lives, there is little definition like that. They continue to be involved in activities and with people needing all three types of pruning. And this is why mere cost cutting will not get you what you want. Just continuing to do the same activities but doing them "less resourced" will give you less of what you were already not happy with! Not too smart: "We have lackluster results, so we will cut resources in the same areas of focus to get better results." Really?

In your business and in your life, don't just "cut back" and think that you have pruned. *Pruning is strategic.* It is directional and forward-looking. It is intentional toward a vision, desires, and objectives that have been clearly defined and are measurable. If you have that, you know what a rose is, and pruning will help you get one of true beauty.

SUBCATEGORY PRUNING

Pruning not only applies to the big picture, such as pruning toward a vision; it also applies to smaller categories of activities, in the little branches of life and business as well. I refer to this as subcategory pruning or micropruning. For example, let's look at how micropruning could be applied to a weekly meeting of an executive team, department, or project team. These meetings are about routine matters—you aren't firing anyone, eliminating business units, or reinventing key strategies—but the team might still benefit by taking some time to ask itself questions in the three pruning categories:

- What ways are we spending time in these meetings that are good and helpful but not the best use of our time together?

For example, "Let's cut out going around the table and reporting in from each department on the status of every project. We need these updates, but we can get that information in an e-mail. Let's use our time to focus on what can only happen if we are all together."

- What do we do here that is sick and not getting well?

    For example, "We have tried repeatedly to use these times for forecasting, and it just never works. We can't get the information we need as the discussion progresses, and even though we have tried, it is confusing and a waste. Let's stop using this meeting to do that."

- What is dead and just taking up space?

    For example, "All of the reviews we go through on operations from the previous time period don't add value to our purpose here. It is not moving anything forward. Let's stop doing that."

The idea here is that it is not just an entire company or life that needs pruning; the devil is in the details as well. If people could learn to say things like, "We only have a little time, let's stay away from certain issues and focus on what we can do something about," or "Let's use our time in a good way," the resources of time and energy would be better spent.

In the personal realm, I have also taught this method to couples, and they see immediate changes. One couple reported back that they changed their weekly "date night" as a result:

"We used to take the time to have a date night every week, get a babysitter to spend time together apart from the kids. But, we would go out and end up talking about the kids, running the house, and all the things that we were trying to get away from. We lost the benefit of date night and were coming back not feeling very refreshed or renewed with each other and our relationship.

"So, we asked ourselves about the three categories and decided that there were good but not best ways to spend our time, things that we talked about that got us into conflicts that were not getting well, and some ways of spending our evenings that added nothing.

"Then we decided to make those off-limits. We started having real dates again, like when we were first dating, before kids and the challenges of running a household took most of our attention. We remembered what it was like when we first met and every minute gave more life to our relationship. And we did the things we used to do. Now we are looking forward to that night . . . it kind of grounds us now through the week. I know that no matter what is going on, that night is going to bring me energy."

All of your precious resources—time, energy, talent, passion, money—should only go to the buds of your life or your business that are the best, are fixable, and are indispensable. Otherwise, *average* sets in and a meeting or even a date night does not become the rose it was designed to be. How many times have you heard someone walk out of a meeting and ask, "Why do we have these meetings?" Pruning might help that, or it might keep a couple from going to sleep after a date night a little more discouraged about their marriage. Pruning can bring health into the small branches of business or life as well as the big.

IN LIFE AS WELL

One last reminder about pruning and necessary endings. The concepts apply to all of life, business and personal. Although this is a book contextualized in business and leadership, the concepts here will apply in every area of your life where you are spending yourself and your resources. And I say that not only as a helpful hint for you to look at all of life as a place for endings, but for another reason as well.

The bigger issue is that your character as a person works best when you are "integrated." In my book *Integrity*, I talked about how the word *integrity* comes from the Latin word meaning "whole," and how business and leadership work best when a person has an *integrated* or whole character. *They are then running on all cylinders and are the same person on the job as they are at home.* They are able to use all of their capacities in both places and accomplish their vision.

I have seen leaders who are not facing the personal issues that they need to face, and as a result, their performance in both business and their personal lives is being held back. You are one person, and as you integrate all of what it means to be a whole person, you will do better in every area of life. And learning to prune and execute necessary endings are important aspects of being a whole person.

For this reason, I recommend that as you go through this book, you see it as not just about business or leadership but about your whole life. In that way, it is about *you*. You are the one who is doing business and also doing life, and if you change and become a person capable of executing necessary endings, you will not only have better business performance, but you will also be less likely to raise failure-to-launch kids or be stuck in some other area of life.

So, with that, let's get oriented to the idea of seeing necessary endings as a normal part of life instead of as a problem and find out how to execute them.

CHAPTER 3

Normalizing Necessary Endings: Welcome the Seasons of Life into Your Worldview

I was introduced to Blair by a friend of mine on a golfing trip. "So what do you do, Blair?" I asked.

"I am in bonds!" he said, with an upbeat kind of energy sparked by the question. I remember thinking, *Must like it, that bond work.*

"It's more than that," our mutual friend said. "He is one of the top guys in the country right now."

"Wow, that's cool," I said. "Have you been in bonds for a long time?"

"No, not too long," he said. "It's a second career for me. I was in chemical manufacturing for a long time, and then made a switch a couple of years ago."

"And you got to the top in a second career that fast?"

"Yep, it just all worked," he said, an answer that seemed to have a lot of drop-down menus behind the headline. So the performance coach part of me had to hear the rest of the story, as I know that those sorts of changes don't happen without a lot of good things occurring in a person.

"How did you go from manufacturing to bonds? What was that move like?" I inquired.

"Well, I owned a company that sold a chemical process that had the writing on the wall, so I got out just in time," he said. "Or after it was time, depending on how you look at it."

"What do you mean the 'writing on the wall'?" I asked. "What kind?"

"The process that we sold looked like it was becoming less and less needed because of other changes in technology, and our sales were reflecting that. It was becoming obsolete. As I looked into the future, it was not looking good. So, I sold it. Got out, did some classwork, studied, got a securities license, and here I am."

"OK, but you aren't twenty-five with a backpack and a bike going to class. Wasn't that a big deal?" I wondered out loud as I pictured what kind of disruption this must have been in the middle of life.

"Yeah, it was. Mortgage, kids headed for college, and I had sunk a *lot* [*heavy sigh, eyes closed*] of money into the company. To make the change and to watch all of that go away was not easy. But, I knew, after a lot of sleepless nights, a lot of effort, going over it and over it trying to find a way to make it work, that it had no life in it. As hard as I had tried to make a go of it, I had to get out and do something different."

And he did. And he had found life again in his new career.

He told me, though, there had been many temptations to keep believing that the old business could turn around, and many times he kept investing good money after bad—second mortgages on the house, outside money, the whole thing. But he finally came to what we will examine later as "the moment." *There was a moment in time where he knew that it was "time" to get out.* He had to end it and move on.

What impressed me was not only his courage to begin a whole new career at his stage in life, but also the contrast to another friend whom I was watching in a similar situation but with a much different outcome. Geoff was also in a business whose time had come and gone with changes in technology, but he was still holding on. His company was tied to satellite technology that enabled multiple locations of companies to communicate with each other, but Web technology was quickly closing in. Having made a fortune in another industry, he had bought this company with a lot of promise, but over the last few years, their niche and advantage were disappearing.

Instead of waving the white flag and morphing into something new, he was determined to make it work. He had convinced more than half of his board that it would, and they were continuing to look for money to keep it going. He still maintained that undaunted sense of what he called the leadership trait of "hope," and he was steadfast. But in my mind and in the minds of the other members of his board—not to mention potential investors, who were increasingly not returning calls—what he was calling hope was only an empty wish. He was headed for a crash, and it was just a matter of time.

What was the difference between Geoff and Blair? Was it brains? Was it experience? Was it market savvy? No, it was none of those. They both possessed equal amounts of talent and brains. It was something that goes deeper.

The difference was how comfortable they were with endings, which enabled Blair to see what needed to be done, and made Geoff keep the blinders on.

Blair overcame his internal conflict and initiated an ending when he finally saw that it was time, and yet my friend Geoff had hit a wall. Even the most gifted people and leaders are subject to feeling conflicted about ending things, so they resist that moment of truth. And not only do they resist, they sometimes cannot even see. Thus they find themselves crosswise with the very nature of life itself.

MAKE ENDINGS NORMAL

In the last chapter, I asked you to use a gut check to examine your feelings about pruning, to come to terms with your previous beliefs about endings, and to honestly assess where your internal resistances lie. This is the first step to moving forward. The second step is this:

Make the endings a normal occurrence and a normal part of business and life, instead of seeing it as a problem.

Then and only then can you align yourself well with endings when they come. It has to do with your brain and how it works.

If a situation falls within the range of normal, expected, and known, the human brain automatically marshals all available resources and moves to engage it. But if the brain interprets the situation as negative, dangerous, wrong, or unknown, a fight-or-flight response kicks in that moves us *away* from the issue or begins to resist it. Execution stops or automatically goes in the other direction. Put into the context of endings, if you see them as normal, expected, and *even a good thing*, you will embrace them and take action to execute them. You will see them as a painful gift. But if you see an ending as meaning "something is wrong if this has to happen," you will resist them or fight them long past when they should be fought. Endings have to be perceived as a normal part of work and life.

Unlike my friend Geoff, Blair had no conflict other than the need to work through the normal painful process that it takes to get to the "moment." He had tried to make his business work, numbed himself at first to the reality, protested and fought it by trying other strategies, turning up the crank and tried even harder, looking for new customers, etc. etc.—really rallying and pushing. He, like any other good leader, was embracing the problem and tackling it head-on. That is perseverance and a good trait. It is essential and causes businesses to be rescued out of the jaws of defeat every day.

But, *he was also able to admit when more effort was not going to bring about a different result.* That is the *moment*, when someone really gets it and knows that something is over. You have seen the scene in the movies when the patient dies, the doctor looks up at the clock, quotes the time of death, breathes a heavy sigh, pulls off her gloves, and walks out the door. The doctor has done everything in her power to avoid this outcome, but when the monitor goes to the steady beep, she accepts what is normal, albeit unwanted, and moves on to try to save the next life.

Likewise in business and life, there comes a moment when that reality must be seen and grasped. Blair was able to grasp it because it fit into his worldview, that sometimes things end. His view of normal included the fact that "this happens sometimes." It is just as important a leadership and personal trait as perseverance. As a result of it, he could take the moment and move on. Now he is at the top of another field. If he could not have done that, he could still be at the bottom of the old one, trying very, very hard and talking to the hundredth group of investors.

Geoff, on the other hand, does not view endings as a normal part of the way the world is. In his head, if something is not working, the only option is to "solve the problem" or "work on the strategy or sales." His worldview does not enable him to ask, *Is this thing over?* He is blind to the fact that his business is in a product line whose time has passed; instead, he thinks the team just needs to work harder or better. The truth is that *there is no problem to be solved, other than to get a new set of problems.*

This does not mean that Geoff's company has to die completely, but it will not survive if Geoff doesn't end their current product emphasis and morph it into something new and different. But he cannot do that because he is in conflict with endings in general. He sees them as failure instead of sometimes a natural occurrence.

Certainly I am not saying that every time something is not working, it should end. In fact, it is usually the opposite. As I said, most good ideas have problems and hit obstacles, and leadership takes them through the crises and struggles to success. That is why we need turnaround experts.

But there is a time, a moment, when it *is* truly over, and if that is not in your view of life, you can miss the right time to get out and to turn your attention to something different or new. In an upcoming chapter, we will look at a paradigm for diagnosing when to have hope and when to give up, but for now, here is your assignment: take a look at your worldview, and see if you see endings as a normal part of life, to be fought if they show up before their time but to be embraced when their time has come. Let's look at three organizing principles that will help you make endings both necessary and normal: first, accept life cycles and seasons; second, accept that life produces too much life, and third, accept that incurable illness and sometimes evil are part of life too. Taken together, these three principles will help you to make peace with endings, so that when their time has come, you will be able to do what you need to do.

1. Accept Life Cycles and Seasons
Life is composed of life cycles and seasons. Nothing lasts forever. Even the ceremonial liturgy of marriage, a lifelong commitment, acknowledges an end on its first day, "till death do us part." Life cycles and seasons are built into the nature of everything. When we accept that as a fundamental truth, we can align our actions

with our feelings, our beliefs with our behaviors, to accept how things are, even when they die.

Everything has a life cycle. There is a time to be born and a time to die, as we read earlier. And in between birth and life, there are many activities, which have their own seasons too.

Each season also has its own set of activities. Spring is about sowing and beginnings. Where there is nothing but a waiting field, the farmer sows seeds in the expectation that they will take root and produce a harvest.

The tasks of spring include:

- Cleaning out what is left over from the winter's dying plants;
- Gathering seeds;
- Figuring out which fields you are going to work;
- Making sure you have the resources to take you through the year;
- Actual sowing and planting;
- Protecting seedlings from the elements and intruders; and
- Nurturing the vision of the harvest to guide the task.

In summer, things change again. It is time to tend to what has taken root. The tasks of summer include:

- Directing resources to ensure the crops are growing;
- Preventing disease and keeping insects and other pests away;
- Watering, fertilizing, and pruning;
- Supporting the plants until they can stand on their own; and
- Monitoring, managing, and protecting the crops for the future.

Fall is harvest time:

- Acting with urgency to get crops out of the field before they rot or are damaged by rain or the cold of winter;
- Gathering the harvest completely, not leaving anything in the field;
- Harvesting with efficiency and watching the costs; and
- Harvesting with care so you don't destroy the field in the process.

In winter, everything dies, though preparations continue. The tasks of winter include:

- Getting the financials in order;
- Squaring accounts with lenders for last years' crops and lining up next year's money;
- Repairing equipment and getting it ready for next year;
- Preparing fields for the upcoming year; and
- Reviewing the successes and failures of the past year and tweaking things to do everything better next year.

The problem comes when we do not accept or we willfully ignore these seasons. One classic example is the entrepreneur who begins a business through "sowing seeds" into a market: making calls, meeting people, investing seed money, starting-starting-starting. Every aspect is *generative* in nature. That is the first season.

The business takes root. Summer comes. Now you have a real plant, not a start-up. Now you have a business that needs to be managed, guided, nurtured, developed, protected, trimmed, watered, and so on. That requires leadership and management, skills a lot of entrepreneurs don't have. *Or at least they resist developing because they have not come to grips with the reality of the seasons.* They think all of life and business is a start-up. "More, more, more," is their mantra. That can kill a business that could have had a very good life if someone had seen that sowing had to stop and operating had to begin.

At other times, the end of summer is not seen, and there is no urgency to harvest what has been grown. There is much low-hanging fruit in the business, but the management phase has become the way that everything is always done, the "new normal" instead of a season. This often makes a company ripe for a takeover. Deep-pocketed investors look at the business and see a lot of harvest that is not being captured because management is too busy "tending" to business, a summer activity, instead of moving on to a fall harvest.

Then, finally, harvest season ends, and it is time to shut down and exit that line, strategy, sector, or whatever. But the ones who don't believe in seasons think that it is going to last forever. Real estate developers, for instance, who don't believe in life cycles, go long on land when the market is up, thinking "we can mine this field forever." They build big infrastructures with huge overhead in the boom harvest times (remember the dot-com days) and then, when the days get short, they are caught without enough resources to keep the lights on. They just did not believe that a winter would ever come.

So believe in life cycles and seasons. They are real. Therefore, when the days get shorter or it is time to change, you will not think that "something is wrong," but you will accept the change as readily as a farmer accepts the turning of the calendar. Then you will be able to end the previous season's appropriate activities and move to the next. Endings are easier to embrace and execute when you believe something normal is happening.

That lesson learned helps boards move founders into other roles and bring in seasoned management. They do not have to approach it as if the founder is failing. It helps CEOs make tough decisions also, knowing that they are aligning their business with the natural order that they see unfolding before them. It makes letting go of a long love affair with a product line or a brand possible.

Blair implicitly believed in life cycles and seasons, and he saw that the long harvest that he had enjoyed for so many years was about to end. It was time to shut down and get out while the assets and revenues that were left still had some value. But more than capturing value from what was left, the real task was to get to a field that had some harvest in its future.

And when he moved to selling bonds, he acted in accord with the new seasons. He accepted the tasks of winter, the death of his old business, and "retooled." He studied a new field and got his license. He cleaned the farm, getting rid of everything from the old business that would slow him down, including overhead and debt. He was truly making room for the new. That is what letting go looks like.

Later he began to do the tasks of spring. He went out to sow. He made his calls, worked his contacts, and went looking for new prospects to plant in his new field. Sowing, sowing, sowing. As he landed them, though, unlike a lot of hyper sales types, he tended them as spring turned to summer. He nurtured those relationships and grew them. Slowly the trust grew and the relationships grew, but he did not just keep tending; he moved to making sales, to harvesting those relationships. And harvest he did.

Meanwhile, my other friend is still stuck. He is trying to make something work that is not going to work because its time has passed. And he will continue to try until the bankers and the investors come change the locks. It happens, and often it happens because someone doesn't have a worldview that normalizes endings, which are built into the universe itself: life cycles and seasons.

And it is not only in business. Many marriages, for example, fail because the couple does not make the shift from spring to summer. Spring, the sowing time, is new, exciting, forward-looking, risky, stretching, and enlarging of both people. But after a while, the relationship has to be tended to—the tasks of summer. Some people do not make that shift, wanting the sowing to continue, and they become disillusioned, or in the alpha-male version, continue to sow elsewhere. Serial sowing becomes a pattern, and over a number of years, no relationship equity, no trust, is ever built. If they could see that sowing ends and the work of tending begins, they could harvest an incredible relationship that lasts for many more seasons.

Here are some questions to ponder about your business and your life that may help you to see if your worldview and subsequent activities are taking seasons into account:

- Do I accept that endings are natural?
- Am I, like a doctor diagnosing, always asking what season I am in?
- Do I resist the endings required for changing seasons? If I believed in life cycles and seasons, would I stop resisting?
- Am I hanging on to an activity, product, strategy, or relationship whose season has passed? What tasks do I need to change to enter the new season?
- Am I sowing when I should be tending?
- Am I tending when I should be harvesting? Am I trying to harvest in a field where winter is clearly setting in?
- Is it winter, and am I ignoring the retooling and planning that is timely for now?

In the language of Ecclesiastes, are there situations in business or in life where you are trying to birth things that should be dying? Trying to heal something that should be killed off? Laughing at something that you should be weeping about? Embracing something (or someone) you should shun? Searching for an answer for something when it is time to give up? Continuing to try to love something or someone when it is time to talk about what you hate?

2. Accept That Life Produces Too Much Life

One reason pruning is needed is the fact that the bush produces more buds than it can bring to full maturity. Any bush that is alive and thriving is producing more and more buds every cycle. And any person or business that is thriving is doing the same. Life begets life. That is normal. But it can be too much, as well. This second principle will make pruning normal for you as you accept the reality that life produces more:

- Relationships than you can nurture;
- Activities than you can keep up with at any significant level;
- Clients than you can service all in the same way;
- Mentors who once "fit" but whose time has past;
- Partners whose time has past;
- Product lines than you can focus on;
- Strategies than you can execute; and
- Stuff than you have room for and can store.

So by definition you are going to have to be in the letting-go phase all through life. There is a reason that the term "spring cleaning" came into existence and morphed to mean more than just cleaning, an overall organizing and throwing away of accumulated "stuff." We need it both for quantitative and qualitative reasons.

Quantitatively, we gather more along the way than we have room for. I recently read that Bill Gates quit Facebook because he had too many friends. He was quoted as saying he had "trouble figuring out whether he 'knew this person, did I not know this person.'

It was just way too much trouble so I gave it up" (news.ninemsn. com, July 26, 2009). I don't know why he was burdened by that, as big numbers do not normally send him running, but you get the idea. But quantitatively, your life and your business are going to do the same thing. Just time and activity alone brings more relationships and activities than you have time to service. As a result, they overload the tree and its resources, and you don't have enough of you to give to them. They crack the system as it is overloaded.

Qualitatively, you can't pour yourself into any of them with much depth. When the numbers are too high, quality suffers. I love it when I hear leaders finally figure out that they are not investing enough time in some of their key relationships or direct reports, because they are trying to interface with too many activities or people. They have realized that their success depends on having the time and energy resources to go deep with a few relationships, and they have to end the wish to go deep with everyone, as it leads to skimming the surface with almost everyone.

The truth is that high-functioning people have many, many relationships, and many, many activities. That is a *good* thing. According to brain research and theory, we seem to have a capacity to really manage about 140 to 150 relationships. Obviously not all to the same degree, but the system can handle that number, apparently. Who knows if life on the Internet and social networking will cause that capacity to evolve and get larger as we use it, but it is substantial as it already is.

But it is also true that the high-functioning people who have extensive networks and relationships that really work well are also very, very good at *not* having some, as well. They prune them. High-performing salespeople prune their contact lists for quality. Smart companies prune their customers, focusing on those who deliver the most profitability with the fewest resources. Businesses prune activities and alliances, and individuals drop out of some social ties.

These people have accepted a reality—that they generate more activity than they can fruitfully handle. So they can cut these ties without feeling that "something is wrong" or that they are "being mean to someone." They respect the fact that there are limits to what they can do, to whom or what they can invest in.

Successful business leaders face this truth all the time. Starbucks has had a lot of life in the past years. And what does anything that is alive do? It creates more buds than it can sustain. So this year news came out that said they were closing down hundreds of stores. Who knows what all went into getting more stores than they or the market could nurture, but it sounds as though the decision to cut some of those buds may be getting in line with the way that things naturally fall out. Apparently, someone there has a worldview that includes the reality that sometimes you have more buds than you can grow. Often, when that occurs, the stock price goes up. As Anne Mulcahy, Xerox's chairman and former CEO, recently remarked, "One of the most important types of decision making is deciding what you are not going to do, what you need to eliminate in order to make room for strategic investments. This could mean shutting down a program. It could mean outsourcing part of the business. These are often the hardest decisions to make, and the ones that don't get nearly enough focus" (*McKinsey Quarterly*, March 2010).

Come to grips with this truth, that your life and your business produce more buds than you can nurture, and you will end some things more readily and easily. It won't register as so traumatic, nor will your brain resist as if something is wrong.

3. Accept That Incurable Sickness and Evil Exist

Your business and your life will change when you really, really get it that some people are not going to change, no matter what you do, and that still others have a vested interest in being destructive.

Once you accept that, some very necessary endings get much easier to do. But until then, you might find yourself laboring much longer than you should, still trying to get someone to change, thinking that one more coaching session will do the trick—or one more bit of encouragement, or one more session of feedback or confrontation. Or worse, one more concession.

I have watched well-meaning people literally waste years and millions of dollars trying to bring someone along who is not coming. And often the person may have lots of other talent that the leader doesn't want to lose, or he likes the person so much that he is willing to try over and over again. I watched one COO have a breakthrough moment when, after the umpteenth time he'd attempted to get a marketing person to perform, he finally just scratched his head and admitted, "He just thinks the wrong thoughts." The COO had finally given up and was able to end the misery soon thereafter. But for about a year, he had been trying to get the marketing guy to "see." The marketing guy was very gifted in his work with people but had grandiose ideas and plans that did not work, even while he ignored the diligent blocking and tackling that was needed. He was trying to throw the "Hail Mary" pass when he should have been trying to consistently advance the ball a few yards. The COO tried over and over to get through but couldn't. We don't even have to explain the ways this happens in people's personal lives. It is too obvious, if you just notice the lunchtime discussions.

In an upcoming chapter, we will spend considerable time on how to diagnose the people who are worth your investment of time and trust, which ones may be willing and able to change and improve and which ones won't. The ability to perform this diagnosis is one of the most valuable skills you'll ever learn. So hold on. But for now, come to grips with the fact that some people—no matter how much you give them or how much you try to help them improve their performance in business or in their personal lives—are not going to change. At least not now, and not as a result of anything you are doing. Accept it, and it will get easier to take the necessary steps to make an ending. You will go from being in shock or in denial to asking yourself the right question: what am I dealing with here?

Similarly, as we have mentioned, some businesses, strategies, visions, tactics, or products are too sick to recover and need to be scrapped. We will discuss that diagnostic path as well, but again for now, accept terminal illness and failure as a *valid* possibility. The best performers know how to fail well. They see it, accept it, and move on. They do not keep beating the dead horse, or worse, riding the one with the broken leg. They can call it quits, wave the white flag, and go forward.

A DIFFERENT UNIVERSE

This chapter has been about getting in line with reality. Many people wish for a different universe than the one in which we live. They want one where every day is harvest time and there are no long laborious summer months to go through in order to get there. And when the harvest is ripe and they are thriving, they want no approaching winters where they see that the harvest is over and a cold death is looming.

Also, they want a world where they have no limits. They want to believe that they have enough time and energy to gather people, products, and activities infinitely and never have to end any of them. They do not want it to be true that at some point, they run out of time and energy and have to make hard choices. They want a limitless life where time and space are not realities.

And they want a world where every person is committed to being good and getting better. In this world, if they try to help someone long enough, that person will improve, wake up, and get it. They do not want this universe, the one we really live in, where some people just don't change and still others truly want to hurt you.

But this is the only universe we have, and in it all three of these realities exist. Successful leaders are very much at one with those realities, and when they come upon one of them, their brains do not send signals saying something is wrong. They are aligned and integrated people who are friends with reality. So when one of these realities appears, their brains see these situations as normal, although sometimes painful, and move toward them decisively and with courage and hope. And they are always wisely asking, "What kind of situation do I really have here?"

They know that if they execute the ending of one season's tasks and get on to the next one's, good things can occur. They know that if they cut some relationships and activities away, others will flourish. And they know that if they give up on trying to change someone who doesn't want to change or is not ready, they will have helped that person get one step closer to seeing reality, and they will have freed themselves from the person's negative patterns. So they take that step with love, certainty, and resolve. As we go forward, we will look at some of the particulars of how to create these kinds of endings. But first, make sure you have accepted the real universe where you live and work. Reality is tough, but as Woody Allen said, reality is "still the only place to get a good steak." And have a good business, and life.

CHAPTER 4

When Stuck Is the New Normal: The Difference Between Pain with a Purpose and Pain for No Good Reason

L ife and business involve pain. Sometimes, as we have seen, creating an ending might cause a little hurt, like pulling a tooth. But it is *good pain*. It gives life to you or to your business. Similarly, the rosebush snaps back when it gets pruned. This book is about taking bold steps to embrace that kind of pain.

But there is another kind of pain, one that should *not be embraced*, one that you want to do everything in your power to end. The pain I am referring to here is misery that goes nowhere. That is not normal, and when it happens, it is time to wake up. It is time to realize that anytime pain is going nowhere fast, a few things must be occurring.

First, you might have become acclimated to the misery in some way. You have gotten so used to it that you no longer feel it as pain but view it as normal. Pain by its nature is a signal that *something is wrong, and action is required*. So pain should be driving you to do something to end it. But if you are not making moves to end the dull misery of something going nowhere, then you may have told yourself nothing is really "wrong"—*it is just the way it is.* You are stuck with a chronic ache that has started to feel like the new normal.

Sometimes we are stuck for reasons that are truly outside of our control. But more times than we realize, we are not executing an ending because of *internal factors, not external ones.* Neuroscience research shows that your mind actually develops something akin to hardwiring so that you think and behave automatically. So when your hardwiring has adapted to accept some sort of "stuck reality," you will live out being stuck there. It has become "just normal" to be stuck and put up with a situation that awaits a necessary ending.

The good news is that it doesn't have to stay that way. Neuroscience and experience have shown that we can change, and new pathways and maps can be built that change the way we think and the way we perform.

INTERNAL MAPS

When the recent global economic crisis hit, plummeting markets began to affect companies and individuals in ways over which they had no control whatsoever. Financing dried up, customers stopped buying, and the normal course of business completely changed for thousands of companies and for millions of workers. The crisis had a significant impact on how employees in those companies approached their work; it actually changed their internal software. Their focus on the external factors over which they had no control began to change the way they thought about and perceived the world. Many got discouraged or even defeated.

We know from research that this kind of constant focus and attention can actually change the way the brain works; people develop new mental maps or fall into old ones, which then direct their day-to-day activities, their thoughts, and their feelings. If you focus on all of the bad things that are happening that you have no control over, your map of what to do every day changes.

In several industries in which I worked during the economic crisis, particularly ones that were highly sales driven, I began to notice a syndrome very similar to what Martin Seligman termed learned helplessness. It is a condition in which the person adapts to the misery because *they feel that there is nothing they can do about it*. It is totally out of their control. Bad market or bad economy equals bad results. That is their mental map, and they act accordingly. For instance, when the market was really bad, one seasoned performer in the commercial real estate industry confessed to me that he would find himself just driving aimlessly around town instead of completing his trips to the office or the field. Other high performers told me that they had difficulty picking up the phone to make sales calls in the months following the crash.

But I saw something else going on as well. In several of these situations, even when I saw stuckness and an adaptation to the misery as the new normal, I also observed some high performance occurring too, sometimes right down the hall. In other words, same market, same external conditions, yet a different set of behaviors and results. Why?

The difference was in the brains, the mental models, of the ones who were performing versus the ones who weren't.

First of all, those who were not stuck had a different map of the world. Some did not assume that "there are no buyers right now." They thought instead that in the chaos, there were many, many potential customers who needed to be shepherded through the challenging environment and were being ignored. So they got even busier and contacted them. This was true in several industries that I observed, even the "deadest" ones, like real estate.

Second, their focus was different. They did not spend their time and energy focusing on all of the things that were falling apart that they could do nothing about. Instead, they thought hard and fast about what they *could do.*

In a learned-helplessness model, the brain begins to interpret events in a negative way, thus reinforcing its belief that "all is bad." For instance, when someone doesn't get a sale, it means "I am a loser, the whole business is bad, and it isn't going to change." These are called by Seligman and others the three P's. Events are processed in predictable, negative ways: first, as *personalized* (I am a bad salesperson); second, as *pervasive* (everything I do, or every aspect of the business, is bad); and third, as *permanent* (nothing is going to change). You can easily see why this leads to helplessness and inactivity.

But the productive people did not think in a learned-helplessness way. Their internal software was more optimistic, seeing a "nonsale" as just one more number to get past to get to the one that was going to buy and sustaining other such optimistic-thinking paradigms.

Besides the negative thinking of the three P's in the learned-helplessness model, I also saw a troubling pattern in some individuals—*an even deeper sense of loss of control over things that were, in fact, still in their control.* When someone with this vulnerability is put in a position where things that they cannot control, such as the economy, are affecting them, they shut down and do not execute *in the activities that they can control.* This is where it all begins to go downhill.

So one of the interventions that I have found helpful is to have people and teams get at the root of the problem: feeling out of control. I give them this assignment:

- Take a piece of paper and divide it into two columns.
- In column one, write down all the things you cannot control that are affecting you. For example, bad market conditions, credit and financing stagnation, customer freezes on spending, and so on. Now, worry about all of that. Hard! For about ten minutes. Then stop for the day. You can worry about it again tomorrow. It won't have changed much.
- In column two, write down all of the things you do have control over. For example, making calls, getting prospects, getting potential buyers into financing conversations and relationships, recalling customers who did not buy at last year's high prices but could buy now that prices have dropped, and so on.
- In teams, begin to share, brainstorm, and take action on the things you can control during the rest of your hours at work.

The results are often powerful, because this exercise gets to the root of the problem in the mental map: control. When the map says that nothing you do matters, then you stop focusing on the things that you do have control over, things that actually do matter and that can make a difference. But when you regain control of yourself, strong results can be obtained, even in crummy environments. I got one letter from a wife in the midst of the economic crisis saying "Thank you. You gave me my husband back." So here's the lesson:

Our brains drive our behavior, and it is very possible for our brain hardware and software, the mental maps, to keep us stuck. The good news is that it can be changed with a little focus and a little work. And as true as it was in the context of the financial crash a few years ago, this news is just as true in the context of necessary endings.

So now we get to the next step in the process of making necessary endings a part of your repertoire. First, I asked you to look at how you felt about pruning in general. Next, I asked you to begin to normalize endings. And now the third:

---

*Identify the internal maps that keep you from the endings
you need to execute.*

In the beginning of the chapter, I said that pain is supposed to move us to do something. If you have ever held your finger over a lit candle, you have seen this law in action. But sometimes people get stuck in a type of misery in which they are *prone more to inaction than action.* Learned helplessness and other dynamics can keep you from making the endings you or your business need to make. You can get paralyzed. So let's see how these dynamics work.

EXAMINE YOUR INTERNAL MAP

As we saw above, if your brain senses that something is the way it is supposed to be, it begins marshaling resources to initiate action. But if it senses that something is wrong, which registers as an "error," it moves against or flees whatever it sees as wrong. That is why it is so important for you to have a worldview that sees seasons and life cycles as normal, so your brain will not register them as errors and fight them. Now we are going to look at some other belief systems or internal maps that might be keeping you stuck and too paralyzed to make endings.

Normally, when you see that something is good to do, you will do it, *unless your software says that it is not good to do.* Normally, when you see that something is right, the brain moves forward to execute it. Your brain exercises something psychologists call conflict-free

aggression. (Not bad aggression, as we normally cast it, like vio-
lence), conflict-free aggression is energy that is free to take action,
not hampered, so you can function. If you have ever been depressed
or anxious while you tried to concentrate or reach a goal, you know
what it is like when this ability is missing or unavailable to you.

If aggression, initiative, or energy is without conflict, it is free to
move you to perform functions like these:

- To sense what is really going on around you;
- To think logically;
- To think abstractly;
- To exercise good judgment;
- To concentrate;
- To see dangers realistically;
- To see reality;
- To make decisions;
- Then, to act on all of the above.

If there is an internal conflict, however, or what neuroscien-
tists are now calling perceived errors, then the action shuts down
and you move away from the decision or protest it. You don't see it
clearly and can't act when you do. Where does this conflict come
from? Your internal software, *which is composed of your belief systems
about endings and your past experiences with them.*

Remember Ellen, the newly appointed executive I described in
chapter 2? She saw clearly what was right to do for the business.
But *her software said that it was not right for her to hurt someone.* Her brain's
operating instructions saw hurt and harm as the same thing, which
prevented her from moving decisively.

Another leader I worked with told me that when he interacted
with a particular direct report, he often found himself unable to
think or to concentrate. As we probed further, he recognized that

these feelings came up whenever they got into a discussion about trimming staff from that person's department. It was a department that this leader formerly headed; he still had a lot of relationships with the people there and felt deep loyalty to them. The very thought of an ending that would affect the people he cared about made his brain slow down. His conflict with an ending affected the kinds of functions I listed above, and he was freezing up. The sad thing was that he was actually working against himself, for if he had all of his brainpower available to him at those moments, he might have been able to find ways to save many of them—but not without his creativity and insight, which was shutting down. When we removed that way of thinking from his mental map, he was able to get moving again.

Here is a key question to help you get a handle on what might be preventing you from acting: What are the mental maps that keep you from executing a necessary ending?

To help you answer it, I'll list some of the kinds of thinking patterns that I have seen in lots of people, even very high-functioning leaders. See if you identify with any of them, then become consciously aware of how these maps drive your behavior. One of the big first steps to rewriting your brain's software is awareness.

One more thought about mapping and internal software. Maps are built up in myriad ways. All of your past experiences with endings go into that computer called your brain and become a part of who you are. As we review each of the maps that follow, notice how the threads of past experiences are woven throughout.

FIVE INTERNAL MAPS

Let's look at some of the most common maps that keep necessary endings from happening: having an abnormally high pain threshold, covering for others, believing that ending it means "I failed," misunderstood loyalty, and codependent mapping.

Having an Abnormally High Pain Threshold

"So what is my problem?" asked Dennis, a CEO in tech. "Do I just have an abnormally high threshold for pain? Do I just by nature put up with too much?"

"Glad you asked," I said. "The answer is yes, and the bad news is that your board of directors and your P&L don't. So, we have got to get to work on it so you begin to feel the heartburn as deeply as they do."

Dennis was exactly right. He had learned to put up with a lot of misery and was almost numb to it. He knew there were problems, and he was working on them, but if he had not gotten so used to putting up with people's problems, he would have acted much sooner. He had some internal software that said to him, just like what some parents say to kids when they hurt themselves: "Oh, stop whining. That doesn't hurt." Gradually a child gets to the point where he can't really weigh his own feelings anymore and instead learns that even when he is hurting, well, "it doesn't hurt."

Dennis was like that. He had had formative experiences in his life in which he had to put up with a lot of pain at the hands of others. As a result, he learned to become responsible for their problems and to negate his own emotional responses to them. He had been systematically talked out of his gut feelings, his perceptions, and his ability to weigh them.

Having become so accustomed to a high level of pain in his upbringing, his brain now registered it as normal, and he was numb to the poor performance of others and how much he was stomaching for them. He just tolerated difficult situations long past when they should have been dealt with. My main work with him was twofold: first, to get him in touch with and aware of how much he tolerated negative things, and second, to get him to be more *instantly* aware of how he really felt about the poor performers who stood between him and the goals. I had him sit and tune in to himself after meetings, reviews, updates, and conversations with the team. Gradually, he began to notice. Finally, one day in one of our sessions, he came out with it.

"I am getting more and more bugged with Peter," he said. "I am sick of how long this project is taking him. I have been asking him for over a year to get us where we need to be on this, and he still is at about step two."

"So what are you going to do?" I asked.

"I think I am going to go create some of that urgency you talk about," he said.

And he did. But not until he saw how his software had been written to negate, minimize, put up with, and carry a lot of pain, all the while telling him it was "not that bad" or he "could buckle up and keep going." Soon after, he made some significant changes in the company, not only replacing some people, but also putting an end to the option of nonperformance (a concept we will talk about later). His misery ended.

Covering for Others

Akin to having an abnormal pain threshold is the map that drives some people to take too much responsibility for others. I often tell leaders that many of them have a problem just because of who they are: nice and responsible people. Nice, responsible people got where they are by caring about others and also working very hard and being super responsible, making sure it all gets done.

But they have a vulnerability, also. They often got to be so responsible in their "mapping" years because they were the superstars of families or other systems and learned that it *all depended on them*. They usually covered for others, taking on the responsibilities of someone else—often a sibling, sometimes a parent—who was not pulling his load; over time they just got used to doing that. Recently I talked to a woman who said she remained too long in situations and relationships that were not good for her based on a childhood map that was created when she covered for an alcoholic mother by raising her younger siblings.

There are certain benefits to this behavior in the short term, but the long-term consequences far outweigh them. One consequence is that relationships and projects are allowed to go on far past the point when they should have been "fixed, closed, or sold." As a result, goals are not reached and potential is not realized, not to mention the misery of the one who is doing all the work.

Believing That Ending It Means I Failed

Leaders, like most good people, persevere. It is one of the most fundamental character strengths in the human repertoire. Life and success depend on it, in every area, from performance success to relationship success to even our physical health and well-being. Especially with winners and high performers, quitting is never an option.

But there is a toxic version of not quitting. It happens when the label of "quitting" in the big sense is equated with stopping a particular goal or endeavor. In other words, if you quit any one thing, you are a quitter instead of being wise. For example, the map says that ending a particular business strategy means you are a quitter. giving up on a relationship means being a quitter. "If you shut ʒn this project, or quit trying with this individual person, you ᴇ a quitter, and that is terrible," is what the internal map says. Quitting is just bad, period. Always, anytime, anywhere.

Furthermore, the label gets attached not to the project or the individual case, but the self. "I am a quitter," is what goes through the person's head, instead of "I decided to fold on this particular hand. It was stupid to go forward." One of the most important aspects to any high performance is the ability to separate one's personhood from any particular result. Quarterback Peyton Manning does not think he is a loser if he throws one interception or loses one game. His identity is separate from any one result. Likewise, successful leaders are bigger than any individual outcome; their sense of self-worth doesn't depend on its having to work. Their whole self-image is not at stake. They are separate from "the deal."

If leaders are not separate from a particular outcome, then there is real trouble. I have seen many leaders drive companies downward in a relentless, stubborn drive to make a particular vision or strategy succeed, or even a person, so they would not feel like or be labeled a failure. In reality they became much more of a failure because of their failure to fail well. Failing well means ending something that is not working and choosing to do something else better.

Psychology researchers Charles Carver and Mark Scheier make the distinction between "giving up effort" and "giving up commitment." They point out how important it is to realize that giving up on some particular commitment doesn't necessarily mean you have to give up on effort. Instead, that effort can be redirected to another goal worthy of your resources. But some people have maps in their heads that say, "Any giving up is bad." This belief keeps them from endings that should happen. See: C. Carver and M. Sheier, "Three Human Strengths," in *A Psychology of Human Strengths: Fundamental Questions and Future Directions for a Positive Psychology*, eds. L. Aspinwall and U. Staudinger, (Washington, D.C.: American Psychological Association, 2002), pp. 87–102. Sometimes it makes sense to quit a particular project or goal. It does not mean you are a "quitter."

Misunderstood Loyalty
Our most powerful internal maps are our relational ones. In fact, our earliest mappings of the world come from our relationships. This is probably not news to you, but it is very important in terms of endings. You have software that tells you how to negotiate virtu-

ally every aspect of life as it plays out in relationships, and the maps order how you think, feel, and behave.

If these rules come into conflict with any particular ending, then you will be stuck. I worked with a business owner one time who began under a mentor who launched him and brought him up in the business. This mentor was a great gift to him, and without him he probably would not have even gotten started. They worked together in the business for about a decade.

But then, the student grew past the teacher, and it was time for a launch. He had great opportunities before him and needed to take a step, but the mentor relationship was holding him back. He had formed a rule in his head that said to grow up and move on was being disloyal and ungrateful. He could not see how he could separate his business from his mentor and be anything other than a real jerk. So he stalled. He missed opportunity after opportunity. His misplaced loyalty had put a ceiling on his personal potential as well as his business potential. He felt he owed his mentor so much that he could never leave him.

After a lot of awareness, focus, and internal "remapping" he got to a place where he was conflict-free enough to move forward. He could finally see how leaving, moving on, and becoming all that he was meant to be was really a validation of his mentor and that he could be loyal and keep a good relationship with him even if they were not partners. It was rocky for a bit, as most endings are, but with the new map, he could negotiate it well. As a result, he became enormously successful, but about three years later than he should have. One wonders how much he left on the table in those stuck years in terms of money, achievement, growth, and even contentment.

In other instances, the map about the other person can have different content. As we have said, some people, like Ellen, often feel that they will harm people if they hurt them. Or such a person may feel that she will destroy someone's life if she makes a decision that is good for her but requires the other person to take some responsibility for the outcome. This is common in both business and personal lives. It is just one of the truths about life: sometimes we need to do something for ourselves or our business that is not good for someone else, at least not in the short term.

Our decisions might take business away from others or force them to deal with some rejection or loss. But ultimately they are responsible for their own lives, as adults have to be. But if your map says that you are responsible for other adults as if they were your children, then something is wrong with your map, and no doubt some well-needed endings are not taking place.

The map that makes people feel responsible for other people is one of the most ending-delaying maps there is. It usually comes from having been parented in a way that makes the child feel guilty for choices that did not make parents or other members of the family happy. As adults, such people need to learn a new map that says, "I am not doing this 'to you.' I am doing it 'for me.'" There is a big difference.

Loyalty is important, one of the most important character traits we can have. But loyal love does not mean infinite and/or misplaced responsibility for another's life, nor does it mean that one forever puts up with mistreatment out of inappropriate loyalty.

Codependent Mapping

Another relational map is feeling responsible for another person's pain when the enabling is ended. This topic has been so well discussed in addiction and self-help literature that I almost did not include it. But I can't ignore it, as it is one of the deepest, almost pathologically archetypal behavior patterns in the human race. It is as though we are "enabling" as a species. It seems it goes that deep into our imperfect DNA, and rampant in business.

Actually "imperfect DNA" is a good way of looking at this one, *as it is a form of caring gone awry.* People enable others because they care. But this kind of caring is not caring at all and is destructive to the person being helped. It is a toxic dependency. It keeps adult kids dependent on parents long after they should have been independent adults. It keeps addicted spouses and friends addicted long after they should have been allowed to hit bottom and wake up (see chapter 7 on the wise, the foolish, and the evil). It keeps employers stuck with dead weight and paralyzes people's professional growth. It is horrible. And yet it is one of the strongest maps that people have in their heads. So make this distinction in your mind firmly:

There is a difference between helping someone who is disabled, incapable, or otherwise infirm versus helping someone who is resisting growing up and taking care of what every adult (or child, for that matter) has to be responsible for: herself or himself. When you find yourself in any way paying for someone else's responsibilities, not only are you stuck with a delayed ending, but you are probably harming that person.

I do not see this mental map in the DNA of all companies, but I do see it in three instances quite often: (a) private companies that profess "we are family" cultures, (b) family-owned companies, and (c) many nonprofits. In my experience, enabling behaviors happen in these settings to a greater degree than in companies with performance-oriented cultures. A few comments about the pros and cons of these kinds of maps:

First, I love it when a company has a "family feel." It is so great to see a business actually care for its people and create a culture in which people feel they belong to the "family of Acme Inc." It connotes so many good things: loyalty, commitment, community, values, belonging, taking care of each other, et cetera. But sometimes the commitment to being a family gets interpreted in two destructive ways that often remain unspoken. The first one is that "we will put up with you no matter how you perform, and you always have a place here." That should not even be true in a biological family! I tell my own kids that everyone who lives in this house has to contribute. "We will divide up all the chores, and the cost for living here is that everyone has their own chores. OK, first item on the list: mortgage. Who wants that one?" No hands go up. "OK, I'll take that one. What about feeding the dog?" I get more hands for that one, since they know I am serious. But some companies with the "family mantra" don't even act like a normal family that requires everyone who lives in the house to have chores and contribute. So if you are going to be a "family" culture, which is great, then at least don't be a dysfunctional one!

Second, in these companies, it can also be implied that "if you give yourself to us, we will take care of you, almost for life. You have a place here no matter what." That is not implied by the business but by the overall philosophy. Again, not to sound like slumlord Mr. Potter in *It's a Wonderful Life*, who hated "sentimental hogwash" that gave people breaks, this philosophy can be an infantilizing way of thinking, causing some employees to think that the business is responsible for their well-being. They sometimes neglect their own growth, failing to recognize that they need to take responsibility for making themselves more valuable *to this business or any other.* Ironically, this neglect may cause them to be even more dependent on the company.

But if they are developing themselves, their great performance then puts real and good pressure on the company to treat them better than any of the other thousand companies who would die to take them away. In that case, they have a great and healthy *mutual interdependency* that spawns a lot of life and a lot of value for both the employees and company. But to think that they are the company's "children" who will be taken care of no matter what is good for no one.

In the family-owned businesses, the failure-to-launch syndrome can become a business practice. If you are not familiar with that term, it is used to describe people in their twenties or older, who are living with parents and have not been able to successfully launch into adulthood. Certainly there are circumstances in which living with parents makes sense, and I am not decrying that. But sometimes the situation is not good and enables a childlike dependency in an adult. (In some situations, you cannot even call it a *healthy* childlike dependency, as many times these twenty-somethings have no chores, requirements, or responsibilities, nor is their living with parents in service of anything else, like further education.)

But when that dynamic becomes part of the business, then grown kids are allowed to "work" there and sometimes have big jobs because they are family, not because they are performing. It is destructive to the ones who *do* perform, to the one who is not performing, to the business, to the culture, to the family, and *especially to the other employees who work hard and see the nepotism.*

In a similar way, sometimes in these companies, the family feel can also be extended to employees as the same dysfunctional family dynamics become corporate practice. These maps can also be hurtful to all concerned and prevent some significant necessary endings.

Check in with yourself and see if you have any of these relational maps that may be hurting you, your business, or your employees.

PAST EXPERIENCES

Our psychological makeup is a collection of past experiences, and these determine how we think about endings. As we have noted, you were designed to do proactive endings, developmentally, throughout life. But if you had many painful endings or dysfunctional maps of endings in your formative years, you might have difficulty with them now.

I worked with one CEO in the travel industry whose personal history included more than her fair share of early losses. As a result, she could not end almost anything, either personally or professionally. Each time she would think about an ending, she would get a sick feeling inside and back away. When we examined the issue and traced this pattern through her client list, it looked a lot like her dating life. There were clients and companies that she had long since outgrown, strategically, qualitatively, and quantitatively. But she stayed entangled with them for way too long, unable to "break it off."

In other cases, people's development has not provided them with the skills to do endings well. They have never been shown how to have a difficult conversation or to communicate in a way that might even fix a problem so an ending would not have to occur. Their remapping includes filling the holes in that developmental gap, and then they can execute as the conflict or feeling of helplessness diminishes. (We will cover skills building in a later chapter.)

Then, there is the above-mentioned feeling of learned helplessness that many people have from their formative years. Early experiences taught them that when they were in a situation that was causing them misery, there really was nothing that they could do about it other than adapt to it and stay stuck. So that is what they do. That is exactly the opposite of the kind of decision that great leaders make. The great ones step up and make broad, sweeping changes to end some kind of misery and create a new day. People with learned helplessness have more of a "well, I guess we just have to ride it out" mentality that they learned in formative experiences.

But once they become aware that this is an old map in their heads and not the reality that exists around them, they can begin to take action and make the endings needed to construct an entirely new reality, quite different from the one they thought they were stuck with.

Peter Drucker used to say that the great leaders make "life and death decisions," which, as he pointed out, were usually about people. Those are the decisions that cause big directional changes in businesses, where the life or death of the vision depends on someone stepping up and acting. If you have a sense of powerlessness in your situation or a map that doesn't let you act, you won't make life-or-death decisions. Instead, you will tend to accept the slow death of morale, initiative, and sometimes even the business itself. And on the personal side of life, you will miss out on all things vital.

While you cannot control the reactions of the people, the seasons, or the markets, you can always control your response to them—if your internal map shows you that you can.

CHAPTER 5

Getting to the Pruning Moment: Realistic, Hopeless, and Motivated

In *Good to Great*, Jim Collins describes what he calls the level 5 leader, a person who possesses the duality of "professional will" and "personal humility." In one description, he describes the level 5 leader as "humble and fearless," a seeming paradox. While we will get to the humility needed to do necessary endings well, let's first look at the "fearless will" required to step up and make them in the first place. Where does it come from? Are you born with it? Or do you learn it? Most important, can you find it when you don't have it?

Leadership scholars have argued for a long time about whether leaders are born or made. The reality is that the answer is both, as in most nature-nurture debates. Some have fearless genes, it seems. Plus, their experiences make them what they are as well. Peyton Manning is a great quarterback, obviously physically and temperamentally gifted to play football, *and* he and his brother Eli had a great mentor/father to help develop them along the way. Genes, and experiences.

Plus, we also know there is a third major component: *a person's own choices.* That is good news, especially for people who find that necessary endings do not come naturally for them.

But either way, whether born, grown, or pulled up by their own bootstraps via choices, successful people and successful leaders all have one thing in common:

They get in touch with reality.

If you are looking for the formula that can get you motivated and fearless, here it is: *you must finally see reality for what it is*—in other words, that *what is not working is not going to magically begin working.* If something isn't working, you must admit that what you are doing to get it to work is hopeless.

This chapter is about the lifesaving virtue of hopelessness.

The awareness of hopelessness is what finally brings people to the reality of the pruning moment. It is the moment when they wake up, realize that an ending must occur, and finally feel energized to do it. Nothing mobilizes us like a firm dose of reality. Whether it is finally getting an addict to hit bottom and end a destructive pattern or getting a CEO in front of a bankruptcy judge to force the restructuring that he has been avoiding, only reality gets us to do difficult things.

SEEING THE REALITY OF A NEEDED PRUNING
If you comb the leadership literature, one theme runs throughout everyone's descriptions of the best leaders. The great ones

have either a natural ability, or an acquired one, as Collins says, to "confront the brutal facts." This is especially true when it comes to seeing a necessary ending. Drucker scholar Jeffrey Krames puts it this way: "Some managers are able to let go of the past better than others. *Those that have the greatest difficulty abandoning things are often those unable to face reality.* Dr. Sydney Finkelstein, author of Why Smart Executives Fail, conducted a six-year study and identified the two top causes of management failure. Both were directly related to the inability to face reality.

"According to the study, organizations make their greatest missteps when the senior managers' mind-set throws off the firms' perception of reality. The second most common contributor to executive failure involves '*delusional attitudes that keep this inaccurate reality in place*' [emphasis added].

"Perhaps that explains why 'face reality' was Jack Welch's first rule of business. At GE he repeated that mantra time and again and it helped him to make the tough decisions that garnered him such accolades as Manager of the Century by Fortune magazine."

Finkelstein goes on to explain how facing those realities is a key ingredient to executing what Drucker referred to as "abandonment" of what was in the way of tomorrow. What a great way to describe a necessary ending.

Not only is facing reality one of the biggest requirements of success, it is also a significant step in arriving at the pruning moment. As Krames puts it, it's "a key ingredient to executing." Fully embracing reality is not only the "Aha!" of the pruning moment, it is also the *fuel* that can give one the courage to execute the difficult decisions. It can empower you to do what is otherwise difficult.

Getting past denial to the "full embrace of reality," in Krames's phrase, has enormous energy and power to move you into the actions you might have been avoiding, past the avoidance that might have been keeping you stuck. When you are driving down a road that feels wrong, you finally turn around when you clearly see that you have hit a dead end. After the initial shock and discouragement, seeing the bare truth that what we are doing is leading nowhere will get us to change something.

But as Finkelstein's study revealed, many people have a mindset, or "delusional attitudes" that keep the old, inaccurate reality in place. As long as these attitudes are operative, it is difficult for the new, accurate reality to do its fueling work, to provide both the urgency and the motivation needed to execute a change. How to fully grasp reality and get rid of these mind-sets and attitudes is the subject of this chapter.

THE OLD WAY MUST END

Welch Allyn, a ninety-five-year-old U.S. company, is a market leader in medical devices. The business has a long tradition of being an innovator in its field, from its earliest days when Dr. Francis Welch and William Noah Allyn invented the directly illuminated ophthalmoscope. Over the decades, the company has enjoyed employee and customer loyalty as a result of its values-driven culture, leveraging everything good about a family-owned firm. The company's DNA, built around the core value of "be always kind and true," has carried it to consistent growth since its inception. If you have ever been in a physician's office, chances are you have been examined, measured, or monitored by a Welch Allyn instrument and would instantly recognize the familiar blue and green logo.

In that kind of business scenario—sustained growth and profits over decades, enjoyment of strong and stable market share, brand recognition and industry standing, happy and fulfilled employees, and a forever loyal and well-cared-for customer base, it is easy to feel the push to keep going just as you are. "Don't change anything, just don't screw it up." Why in the world would you want to change anything when you have, in ever-increasing measure, what every business tries to accomplish?—being a market leader, having great profits, and being loved by everyone you touch?

You wouldn't . . . *unless your worldview included life cycles and seasons, as well as an experience base that had trained you to know a pruning moment when you saw one and got terrified by it.* That is what happened to Julie Shimer, Welch Allyn CEO.

When Shimer became CEO, she was selected from the board of directors, so she was familiar with the company and its business. But it was not her board experience that had led her to see the pruning moment needed at Welch Allyn. It was being an experienced technology executive who had witnessed and lived through what happens when leaders miss a necessary ending.

Shimer, an engineer by training, began her career at Bell Labs, learning the rigorous process of technology product development and the inherent business dynamics between development and bringing products to market, one of her key competencies. She went from there to Motorola, where she continued her career in overseeing product development and managing various P&Ls. As she explains, it was there that she got her real training in what happens when leaders miss necessary endings and what missing them can do to a company. It is that experience at Motorola and in the wireless industry that is driving what may prove to be Welch Allyn's biggest innovation to date: the introduction of a single diagnostic platform for innovation across all Welch Allyn medical devices.

What does that mean? It means that Shimer is taking the company through a process of ending the practice of having each medical device run on its own operating system, and *creating a single platform for all of them, with one simple user interface.* Never done before, she is basically undoing the technical side of the last 100 years of medical device design, and creating a necessary ending. The result of this change will be that no matter what device a doctor or nurse is using, the interface will look the same as all the other devices they use and will run on the same operating system, or platform. Think iPod, iPhone, iTunes. And like the iPhone, this platform will also include an open architecture available to an unlimited number of outside software developers. That means that software developers all over the world can create applications that will make Welch Allyn devices the industry standard for virtually every aspect of frontline medical diagnosis.

Just as an iPhone can do as many different jobs for you as you have applications for, Welch Allyn will be in a position to drive most of the world of medical devices, a feat that no one else has seen the "moment" to seize. And in a climate in which more and more care is being driven toward the front lines and being delivered by people with lower levels of training, the practical medical need for this is great.

Now to the pruning-moment discussion. *Why did Shimer get it when others had not?* What drove her to the pruning moment where, in Drucker's words, she decided to "abandon the past," and create a necessary ending to ninety-five years of how the company made products? In short, *she lost hope in the old way, even when it was succeeding.* To understand that, you have to go back to the point where she learned to recognize life cycles and seasons and learned to see that if she didn't recognize them, she could lose everything. I asked her that question, and this is what she told me:

The real learning moment came when Motorola missed the coming of digital cellular technology. In the midnineties, AT&T asked Motorola to develop a digital phone. Motorola thought that customers would not accept digital because of the poor voice quality. They had the attitude that they were the market leader, they were doing great, and if they refused, it would not happen. So, AT&T went to

Nokia instead, and Nokia got it. They said, "We'll do it for you." Brand-new in the business, Nokia led the way, ending the era of analog and beginning the new digital era. Nokia took market leadership from Motorola. *Missing the ending of analog in cell phones was a big mistake. I learned through that experience to pay attention when something is over and it is time to create urgency around the new.*

So, when I got to Welch Allyn, I saw the lack of an overall platform strategy. Their strategy was to continue to make more great products with great features. And they did. And Welch Allyn was profitable, year after year. But I could see an end in sight as other parts of the technology world were migrating to platform approaches. RIM was doing it, Apple was doing it, and it was clear everywhere but in medical devices. So, *I began to feel uneasy about the future,* seeing that Welch Allyn was heading down a path that had been successful for a long time but might not be forever. I had seen that happen before and had learned the lesson.

At that point, I hired a strategic planning consultant, and we went into a planning process. We began with an assessment of the market environment, the job we were doing for our customers, our strengths and weaknesses, threats and opportunities. At one point, the consultant asked about the team's *sense of urgency to change as opposed to keeping it going like it was.* We did not yet know what we needed to do, but everyone scored themselves 8 out of 10 or higher on an "urgency about need for change" scale. New product introduction and innovation was stuck, we felt, without a strategic plan, and we had not become opportunistic. Our resources were not aligned with a particular strategy, and we were getting an increasing sense of urgency to have a clear vision of where we were going and get resources aligned.

The breakthrough and the pruning moment came when
we did an exercise where we were to picture an ideal future.
We were asked to describe the "desirable future." We started
with the customer—the doctor or the nurse. We saw that
in their future, they were going to be asked to do more and
more, get paid less and less for every visit, have sicker patients, less highly trained staff, fewer nurses to help, et cetera,
et cetera. *We asked ourselves how to make that future desirable for the
doctors and nurses whom we serve. "How can we make it ideal for them?"*

What we came up with was a diagnostic platform that
could meet the current and emerging needs of frontline care
practitioners. We envisioned a future of health care where
a physician could have a Welch Allyn device or application,
with a common look and feel, that could gather data, move
it, present it to others easily, send it to electronic medical re-
cords. We wanted it to be easy to use for clinicians who are not
IT people. We code-named this scenario WAPPLE—Welch
Allyn Apple . . . Apple for doctors. *That was the moment I saw that
a platform approach would help us reach our ideal future. It was a clear
reality from which I could not go back. I saw that the way we were doing it
could not bring about the future reality that we wanted. We had to change.*

All I could see was how Motorola had missed the digital
transition in phones and lost the lead. I was determined that
that would not happen at Welch Allyn. For nearly a century, Welch Allyn has been a leader in innovation, and now
was the time to really innovate. But it would involve a huge
change, ending our entire existing product line platform,
and moving every Welch Allyn product to our new single
diagnostic platform for innovation. It would be a very big
ending, but if we didn't do it, I knew what the future held.
I had seen it in the phone industry, and did not want it to
happen here. To continue our legacy of being a leading in-

novator, we had to change to a new and much bigger chapter in Welch Allyn's history. But even though it is new, it is also consistent with the DNA of the company as an innovator, and if we did not change, I knew that the innovative DNA was at risk. I could not let that happen. It meant we needed to change to keep the innovative spirit we always had.

Shimer saw the reality that was staring her in the face: *change or die*. And she had a lot of reasons readily available to delude herself if she wanted to use them. After all, Welch Allyn enjoys great market share in many product areas. They have had sustained profits and growth for a long time. The industry loves them for good reasons. That can make you pretty comfortable, unless your understanding of the world includes a realization that no matter how comfortable you are in the fruitfulness of autumn, a harsh winter can, and will, come. She was not afraid of that reality and had seen it happen to Motorola and others. She has chosen reality over comfort. She looked at the world and saw the reality of what platforms are doing, and how Welch Allyn needed to be aligned with that reality. So the pruning moment was right in front of her.

Shimer's leadership is an example of clearly grasping reality and making the necessary ending. Fearlessly. How do you do that?

By getting hopeless about what is not going to work.

The first step that will motivate you to do what is necessary is to see that what you are doing has no hope of getting what you want. When that happens, you will instantly feel an epiphany. You realize that to get where you want to get, you *must* make a change. You really get it that to continue to do what you are doing is hopeless, and then you will begin to see motivation to make a change appear. So hopelessness can bring us closer to fearlessness, as *it does not take courage to stop doing what you know is not going to work.* When you see a train coming, you have fear working for you, motivating you to get out of the way. It just takes a clear dose of the reality, over and over, to confirm that you are going nowhere. It creates its own discomfort, which motivates us to action. It is sometimes the most important step you can take, as it will fuel you to make a move.

But remember, to get there, you have to get honest with yourself and be ready to see hopelessness as if it is staring you in the face. You have to come to that moment with 20/20 vision in order to see it, by doing the work of the previous chapters. To have clear vision, the steps we have already discussed must be in place. Here is a brief review:

1. **Do a gut check to see how you feel about pruning in general and identify any potential intellectual or emotional resistance.** You will not embrace a pruning reality if you have an internal conflict with the idea. Shimer had no conflict with this at all. As she reports, she had asked for it at Motorola and did not get it. But it was well within her comfort level to get rid of what needs to be gotten rid of.

2. **Make the concept of endings a normal occurrence and a normal part of business and life, so you expect and look for them instead of seeing them as a problem.** If you really believe that pruning, seasons, and life cycles are as real as gravity, you will not have to be talked into them; you will always be looking for them.

   Just as a good real estate developer does not expect an up cycle to last forever, Shimer did not believe that sus-

tained market share could go on forever in a tech company that was not ending the old ways of technology and
not morphing to the new way of the world: platforms.
Trains versus airplanes all over again. Wires versus
wireless. The dead or dying has to be moved out, and
that is a normal process. Her worldview expected both
seasons and life cycles. Just as a person plans for retire-
ment, she knew she had to plan for product obsolescence.
Her vision in that regard was corrected to 20/20 by the
Motorola experience before she got to Welch Allyn, enabling her to see it. Do not be surprised by obsolescence:
expect it and plan for it.

3. **Identify the internal maps that keep you from executing necessary endings**. In chapter 4, we listed many of
   the personalized maps that get in our way. As I talked
   to Shimer about these, she said that hers were mostly
   cleared out by twenty-five years of leadership experience.
   She was over the squishy thinking that would prevent
   her from executing an ending, having seen too many
   instances where not executing an ending caused more
   pain than it solved. Ironically, the one thinking pattern
   she had to clear up, she said, was in the opposite direction. The shift she had to make was in her thinking that
   it was going to be easier to get everyone on board than
   it was. She learned that getting movement around such
   a monumental change would take more steps than she
   had foreseen. She thought everyone would instantly see
   reality and jump on board. But fortunately, she did not
   have a lot of internal interference with her own wish to
   pull the trigger. *That is the biggest hurdle for a leader.* The rest
   is strategy and implementation.

So at this point, do a little self-questioning about your eyesight. Is it 20/20 with regard to being ready to see an ending? Are you walking into the possibility for a pruning moment with clear eyes? Remember, your brain will shape reality to fit the maps in your head, so make sure your eyes are clear, not blurred by the kinds of maps we have said can get in the way of seeing when an ending is necessary. If they are, let's get to the other ingredients that get us to the point of seeing reality as it really is.

The stakes are huge. If you can see reality and realize that the lights you see in the distance are a train headed straight for you, you will get motivated and make the changes that will lead to success. But, if you don't and you keep having false hope, you might be signing up for failure or worse. Getting to 20/20 vision so you can see reality is a must.

THE BIG CHANGE MOTIVATOR: GET HOPELESS

Hope is one of the most powerful forces in the universe. With hope, we can endure almost anything, and certainly more than if we lose it or don't have it to begin with. In short, hope keeps us going. *And that is the problem.*

When it comes to seeing reality, almost nothing gets in the way like a hope distortion, in either direction. First, if we are the kind to lose hope just because something looks difficult or bleak, we will accomplish little. Almost anything of value is only accomplished because someone kept going past the moment of thinking "all is lost." That is the nature of heroic leadership and heroic life. As Admiral James Stockdale saw in his POW experience in Vietnam, hope is a requirement for survival and winning. Stockdale's experience reminds leaders that you must recognize and own the brutal facts while at the same time never letting go of the determination that you are going to win, no matter how long it takes. In our dis-

cussion of getting to reality, notice how the time and hope dimension quickly enter into it, as Stockdale mentions.

He says to recognize how bad it is and at the same time keep
hope going, no matter how long it takes. *Hope is always about holding on
when it looks bad and being able to hold on sometimes for a long time.* The time
dimension is a key component, because if it did not require time,
we would have no use for hope. We would already have everything
we want, right now, today. But many times we do not have what we
want right now and have to hold on to hope for quite some time,
and then as we persevere, we succeed.

Amazon, founded in 1994, did not make a profit until 2001.
Investors and the markets were losing hope and giving Jeff Bezos
a very hard time, as he continued to have hope and try to convince
others to have hope as well. Time would help and was built into
his business model. He maintained hope as others lost it, and now
Amazon is still around and thriving. He was right, and the ones
without hope were wrong. So hope is good and requires time as
part of its equation. But . . . that is also *the* problem: Hope buys
time, and spends it.

Hope is designed to give us more time, so that whatever we are
hoping for can come to pass. But because that is what hope does for
us—buys more time and spends it—it sometimes creates problems
if we are not in touch with reality. *In that case, it is hope that keeps us
going down a road that has no realistic chance of being the right road or making
what we want come to pass.* In a false reality, hope is the worst quality
you can have!

Yet sometimes, people keep hoping, in spite of a clear reality
staring them in the face.

As Shimer tells it, reality was right there for all at Motorola
to see. Digital was coming. But their profits gave them the false
hope that they could ride that wave forever. Their market share

fueled the happiness of that hope and led them right into Nokia's shadow. Just as hope can conquer all, *false hope can ruin everything*, as well. What Motorola needed was to see what a hopeless future analog really had and that if they continued to hope that it would sustain them, they were going to be in trouble. That kind of hope was a problem.

False hope buys us more time to spend on something that is not going to work and keeps us from seeing the reality that is at once our biggest problem *and* our greatest opportunity. It is our biggest problem because not seeing the reality that needs to be dealt with is what is in between us and what we desire. And it is always our biggest opportunity because if we see it and grasp it, that reality, we can find a *real way that will work*, one rooted in things as they really are, to get what we desire.

Shimer saw the false hope of thinking that Welch Allyn could continue to have the same success without a platform once a platform world had emerged. She grasped the hopelessness of that plan, put her arms firmly around it, and changed the entire company to get in line with the reality of where the future growth will be. Her hopelessness led her to the strategic planning session that gave rise to the platform. The hopelessness of the reality problem they had led her to possibly the greatest opportunity in the history of the company. This is why it is vital to "get hopeless." It can lead you to everything you want.

And this is not only true for business. I met with a woman who had gotten to the pruning moment in her marriage. She finally realized that her attempts to get her addict husband to dry out, her efforts to talk to him about his drinking, were not working. At last, she was "done." In her mind, the situation was finally hopeless, and it was time to divorce. That was a breakthrough. She was giving up hope that what she had been doing was going to help.

But what she did not realize was that her hopelessness was also a great opportunity to get a new and different plan, one that had a chance of reaching her goal: a sober husband. Just as Shimer did not have to get out of the device business and sell the company when she realized that the old way would not work, I reminded this woman that she did not necessarily have to divorce her husband. The good news she needed to hear was that she was finally in a place to do something that might actually help.

Once she saw that her own strategies were hopeless, she could finally get a new plan that might sober him up. We put a plan together that included a professional intervention, using the leverage of his other significant relationships, professional treatment, and enacting consequences. She implemented it, and it worked. He went to rehab, is sober now, has been for a long time, and there is realistic hope for the future. *But it only came about because she got to the hopeless moment of her former way of operating.* So sometimes hopeless can be about just getting rid of the way that we were going about something, not about the something itself. But we can't get to the new hope of the new plan if we don't face the reality that what we have been doing is not working.

So if hope is good but false hope is not, how do we know the difference between the two? How do we know when to hang on to hope and when to grasp the hopelessness that we need to grasp to do something different? *We need a good diagnostic.*

WISHING VERSUS HOPING

It is imperative that you give up hope if your hope is not hope at all but just an empty wish. But how do we know the difference between wishing and hoping?

When most people talk about tomorrow and wanting something in their lives to be different or to get better, they use the word *hope.* Dictionary definitions of *hope* contain two elements. The first is a "desire or expectation" for something in the future to occur. "I hope this thing turns around." The second is usually "grounds for believing" that something in the future will occur. "She sees some hope because of next year's product line." The real problem is when we have one without the other: *a desire without any grounds.* That is hope based not on reality but on our desires, our wishes.

You wouldn't go to a lender and say, "Our business is in a financial mess, but we hope next year everything is going to turn around. So please lend me some money today." There is no realistic, objective reason for Mr. Banker to do that, now that the credit market has made it more difficult to pass the pain on to someone else. Your hope for turning your business around is "hope defined by the desire"—just because you want something to be true, you hope it will be. It is the same reason that people continue to buy time with false hope and spend it waiting for a dysfunctional person to change, believing that it might happen and hoping that their love will somehow turn this person around. There is no real reason for them to have hope at all, for love by itself has never caused a resistant person to change (see chapter 6 on how to know when this is happening). But year after year, they continue to have hope that it will somehow get better if they just keep on loving. Parents with their adult children, continuously helping them out, spouses hoping that it will get better, and business leaders and bosses wanting something or someone to work out so much that they "keep hope alive" can all fall prey to this pattern, in which "desire defines hope."

On the other hand, you might say to a lender, "Our business is in a financial mess, but we just got the rights to operate in twelve new regions that we did not have before, we hired a seasoned sales manager who replaced the boss's dropout nephew, we got a contract to be one of the suppliers to the NFL, and Yahoo! has agreed to put us on their home page. So we have real hope that by this time next year, we will have turned it around, and we just need some capital to bridge the gap." Then the banker does not have to be an

idiot to continue talking to you. There are real, objective reasons
for the bank to have hope with you, give you the financing, and
hope to make a return on their money as well. Hope is based not
only on desire, but also on real, objective reasons to believe that
more time will help. That is way different from mere desire. Here
is the principle:

---

*In the absence of real, objective reasons to think that more time is going
to help, it is probably time for some type of necessary ending.*

That is the moment when the hopelessness requirement gets
fulfilled: You get it that *other than your desire, there is no real reason to have
hope.* There are no real, objective reasons to continue to think that
tomorrow is going to be good. Does that mean that your dream is
hopeless? Not necessarily. It simply means that you have looked
down the corridor of time and realized that there is no real reason
to believe that your current strategy is going to bring about anything different than it already has or is going to work in the face of
the harshest real facts. As the saying goes, "Hope is not a strategy."
This kind of hope is not worth spending more time and resources
on. It is only buying you the time to continue to make more mistakes. If you are in a hole, rule number one is to stop digging. The
last thing you need is more of this kind of hope.

But if you can get to the wonderful virtue of hopelessness by
seeing that there is no reason to believe that tomorrow is going to
be any different from today, then you finally have gotten to reality.
It is hopeless to continue to do what you are doing, expecting different results. That kind of hopelessness is great. It is the doorway
to getting on the right track.

It is the kind of hopelessness that can motivate a Julie Shimer to take the kind of action that really can bring true hope, the kind of hope that is worth betting ninety-five years of success on. It is the kind of hopelessness that can cause people who are stuck in dead-end relationships to begin to make the changes that can turn the relationship around or help them to move on. While hope is a great virtue, hope in unreality is not. And sometimes hopeless is the best virtue you have, because it can finally get you to the pruning moment. Shimer saw it, and got hopeless. At that moment, everything changed for Welch Allyn.

Perhaps you are at that moment as well. You have been having "hope" that something, or someone, would turn around. Maybe it, or the person, will. To give up hope when there is victory in sight is a mistake. But to hang on to false hope is a fantasy that can end in dismal failure. The question is, how do you know the difference? Is there a key? A formula? Without a crystal ball, are there ways to know when to hold on to hope and when to give it up and have a necessary ending?

That is the subject of the next chapter: when to have hope, and when to get hopeless. What are the real, objective reasons that we can depend upon to have hope, without which we may need a necessary ending? We will soon see, but for now, here is the question for you or your team:

What reason, other than the fact that I want this to work, do I have for believing that tomorrow is going to be different from today?

In the next chapter, we'll take a look at how to answer that question.

CHAPTER 6

Hoping Versus Wishing: The Difference Between What's Worth Fixing and What Should End

The last thing you would want to do is go through a major ending for no good reason. But another last thing you would want to do is to continue to hold on when an ending is needed. To hold on to "hope" when what you really have is merely a wish is to fail to grasp reality. Whether it is the decision to stay in a business or to stick it out with a person, it is a big decision.

But what is worth keeping and fixing, and what should end? How do you know the difference? When does it make sense to have hope, and when does it not? In the last chapter, we saw how one leader knew the difference because her eyes had been opened through her experience in a previous company. She had vowed that she would never let that happen again, so she got to hopelessness and made the necessary ending. She looked at the past and did not want more of it.

But what if you are not in the same situation as Julie Shimer? What if there is nothing in your past that would make your sniffer say, "I have seen this before and I know where it is headed." If you have never faced the situation that you now find yourself in, is there another way to know? Are there ways to know when there is a reason to have hope and when there is not? When to think tomorrow may be better and when to execute an ending? Let's look at some helpful signs that you can rely on to determine whether you have real hope and should carry on or just a wish that may need an ending.

THE PAST IS THE BEST PREDICTOR

My friend told me that his daughter's boyfriend had called and asked him to go to dinner, and he expected the proverbial "asking for her hand" conversation. He wanted some advice on how to handle that question, and I could understand his trepidation. Few thoughts are scarier to a father than wondering, *Will this guy love her, treat her well, and take good care of her?* As a father of two girls, as I look into the future, I could already feel what that must have felt like for my friend.

We talked about how to handle it, and then I said, "After all of that, tell him that you would like to see his credit report and his last two years' tax returns."

"What? You have got to be joking!" he exclaimed.

"Not at all. I am dead serious," I said.

"Why? I can't ask him how much money he makes. That's so intrusive and the wrong message. Marriage is not about how much money he makes."

"Exactly, and money has nothing to do with my suggestion. I don't care about the numbers at all, how much he makes. Tell him to blot them out if he wants. I only care about two things. First, the credit report will give you a peek into how he has fulfilled other promises he has made to people who have entrusted things to him. If he can't be trusted to fulfill the promises he makes with something such as money, which is not nearly as valuable as your daughter, how are you going to trust him with real treasure? I would see a big yellow flag if he has a history of bailing out on commitments he has made to lenders or others."

While my friend was still trying to absorb the idea of asking for a credit report, I homed in on the tax return. "I don't care what the numbers are. *I just want to know if he has done them.* Does he take responsibility for his life and get things like taxes done? If he hasn't, then that is a sign of what your daughter is signing up for in the future: chaos and uncertainty that come from his character. That would be another big warning. No matter what his financial situation is, I would want to know that he obeys the law, has his affairs in order, gets his taxes done, and sends them in.

"So, the message here has nothing to do with money. It has to do with looking at his past behavior in some areas that count: promises, commitments, and responsibility, and then seeing what the track record has been. That is important because *the best predictor of the future is the past.* What he has done in the past will be what he does in the future, unless there has been some big change. You can bet on it," I told him.

I felt a little bit lecture-ish, and could feel myself getting a little amped up, probably because my own daughters were somewhere in my unconscious. My friend thought that asking for a credit report and tax returns somewhat destroyed the storybook nature of the "ask for the hand moment," but I really believed what I was saying. When my daughters' suitors show up, they better be toting some documents.

Sometimes because of great "hope," or desire, we fail to ask the first question that should be asked: *what has occurred before?* What is the history? I would rather his daughter get to the "hopeless moment" now than later, when the IRS or the bank calls and she is liable for whatever they are demanding. Examining past performance could warn her of that kind of future.

What does this mean in your situation? It means that although you might not have dealt with exactly the same situation you are dealing with now and have no previous experience like this one to learn from, you *do* have some experience to learn from: What has happened so far in *this* situation? What you have experienced in this situation is plenty to learn from.

When you ask yourself if you should have hope for this person or business to get better, the first diagnostic is to see what has been happening up to this point. Unless something changes, that is exactly what you can expect to happen in the future. The best predictor of the future, without other variables, is the past.

I worked with a CEO who was in the middle of a significant acquisition of another company. To get it all up and integrated with the current business, he needed to fill the COO role for the new, blended, executive team. This person would be in charge of seeing the integration through. He went through a normal search process, and the headhunters turned up several candidates, and there were a handful of internal candidates as well. One of the internal candidates, Jonathan, had enormous strengths in certain areas, but one glaring weakness. In big projects, he had a tendency to micromanage certain details and lose the big picture. As a result, some big initiatives had languished, even though Jonathan had made progress in specific parts of the program; he was great on going deep in a small circle, but weak on seeing the big circle.

Still, the CEO loved Jonathan's energy, his ability to connect with the employees, his loyalty, and a host of other qualities. This was the person he was most excited about. But it seemed to me that Jonathan's particular weakness, the inability to stay focused on the big picture, was more than half of what this new role required. If Jonathan got bogged down in the details of any little piece of the whole, the big integration would fall apart. And his past behavior suggested that he would get bogged down in the details.

"I think he would be great at this integration," he said. "He could really pull the troops together and get them on the same page. He inspires so much loyalty. Everyone loves Jonathan."

"It is your decision," I said. "But let me remind you of something. Many, many times you have expressed frustration with Jonathan and his tendency to get bogged down and fail to move the big initiatives forward. You love his work with people, but you hate his lack of creating forward motion. You are always upset with the lack of speed, because he gets stuck in the details. That is what you have experienced. Over and over, you have said that to me. And that is a lot of what this job is going to be about. So without something changing in him that we have not seen, that is what you are looking at happening in the future if you put him in charge of this integration. Is that what you want? Because that is what you are going to get. I would bet on it."

The CEO's sudden look of hopelessness gave me hope. He had gotten it. He had gotten to the hopeless moment by looking at the past and projecting it into the future, which is exactly what we need to do to see if we should have hope or not.

When a credit card company decides whether or not to place hope in you and give you credit for another month, it doesn't look at how hopeful or enthusiastic you are to pay them back, or go and visit a psychic. It looks at your past performance in paying people back, and then it knows what to expect you to do in the future. Sometimes it gets it wrong, but most times not. The past does not lie. Of course, you might immediately ask, "Can't someone do better than their past?" *Of course!* As we are about to see. If that were not true, we would all be hopeless. *But the key is this: There had better be good reason to believe that someone is going to do better.* Without any new information or actions, though, the past is the best predictor of the future. You can bet on it.

So here are the first questions to ask yourself about the anatomy of hope, no matter whether you are assessing a person or some aspect of business:

- What has the performance been so far?
- Is it good enough?
- Is there anything in place that would make it different?
- If not, am I willing to sign up for more of the same?

Those four questions may get you to see reality clearly and, if answered truthfully, could keep you from going down a road of certain failure—the failure of the past. They are also *great* questions for a team to ask itself about key people decisions, as well as specific strategies or projects.

THE ANATOMY OF HOPE

When you consider the past and come to grips with the fact that it is hopeless to expect something different in the future, then you have the kind of hopelessness that will motivate you to move from mere wishing to real hope. How do you get to this hopelessness? As we saw above, take the past performance of the person, business, or whatever, and project it into the future:

- Do I want this same reality, frustration, or problem six months from now?
- Do I want this same level of performance a year from now?
- Do I want to be having these same conversations two years from now?

If the answer to these is no, then it is time to ask some other questions that get you to the real anatomy of hope:

- What reason is there to have hope that tomorrow is going to be different?
- What in the picture is changing that I can believe in?

In the previous chapter, I said that the difference between hoping and wishing is that hope comes from real, objective reasons that the future is going to be different from the past. Anything other than that is simply a wish that comes from your desires. So what are the real objective reasons that we can use to diagnose when an ending may not be necessary and we can hang on to hope versus when it is time to get to hopelessness? What is real hope made of? Let's see.

Endings are necessary when there is no hope. But hope is not a virtue to throw away so easily. We want to have it when it is appropriate. It can ensure the next hundred years of success for a tech company or even save a failing marriage. But to know when to have hope, we need some diagnostics to guide us. Let's look at those now.

WHO DESERVES MY TRUST?

I was talking to a wealthy friend one time about the ways that he invests his money, wondering how he made his investment decisions. What industries and businesses did he prefer, and so on? What he said applies to our discussion here. He told me that he does not invest in businesses, other than his own. When he said that, I disagreed, as I knew of several that he had invested in, and I said so.

"Not true," he said. "I did not invest in those businesses at all. I don't know anything about those industries. What I invested in was what I always invest in: the person. In all of those investments, I knew the leader and his or her team, their track record, and their character. That is what I was investing in, not the business. I would not have understood it if they had tried over and over to explain it. Surely I looked at it and tried to understand as best I could, but the real investment was in the people who were running it and whom I trusted."

That is a good way to think about the role of character as we move forward. What kind of person deserves our trust, and when do we believe that someone can change?

What if the Martians invaded Earth and decided to turn us into a cosmic version of the Roman gladiators, only this time they created a golf tournament to see if they would allow humans to continue to exist or not. Let's say they set up a scenario with a four-foot, downhill, right-breaking putt on the fastest green that Augusta National has. They give the humans one chance to make the putt. If we make it, the earth is spared, but if we miss it, they vaporize us and all of our planet's known life forms. We get one chance, and we get to pick anyone we want to hit that putt. What is the hope for mankind? Will we make it to live another day? Are you hopeful? Well, that depends.

It all depends on *who is hitting that putt.*

If it is Jim Carrey, or Oprah . . . find a ride to Venus. You are probably just hanging on to a wish if you stay here. But if it is Jack Nicklaus in his prime, one of the best clutch putters in golf history, don't sell your property just yet. We have a chance, and a good one. The difference all lies in who is hitting the putt.

The first factor to consider in assessing whether or not there's hope for a certain scenario is to ask yourself, "Who am I dealing with?" Character, giftedness, and all of who a person is, the person's makeup, *is* the future. As the saying goes, character is destiny. Maybe if the test were to make someone laugh, we could depend on Jim Carrey. But to make the putt, our destiny is in better hands with Jack. His makeup to bring the future we desire is dependable. His ability is proved, and he has the elements needed. He is more likely to come through than not. So we have a lot of hope. (Now if the Martian test were to make us laugh or to make us cry, Carrey and Oprah would be back on the table.) You can quickly see how important someone's makeup is to the question of hope.

This is often the biggest error that people make in determining whether to have hope or not. They forget to think about whom they are depending on to get it done. Instead, they look at what they want or wish to happen and forget who is holding the putter. The mistakes come in a number of forms when they place hope in someone they shouldn't:

- The person who is not bringing results is really "sorry" and promises to do better.
- The person who isn't performing "gets it" and tells you that she is really committed "this time."
- You want the best for the person and want to believe that he can do it "this time."

There are a lot of different versions of this story, but the bottom line is this: We wrongly put our hope in some promise, belief, or wish that the person expresses, but ignore the clear reality of who they actually are.

I don't mean this in a negative or pejorative way at all, but in a reality-oriented way. The reality is that the person has not produced so far, and *unless something changes*, the future that you can expect is more of the past. Sorry or becoming committed does not make Jim Carrey a great golfer, or make Jack Nicklaus funny.

Recommitment does not make a person who is unsuited for a particular position suited for it all of a sudden. Promises by someone who has a history of letting you down in a relationship mean nothing certain in terms of the future.

Now, none of this implies that they cannot or will not change in the future, as we shall see below. But what it does mean is that up to this point, there is nothing different about them other than wishes to do better. And that is not a different makeup. If your car is broken or does not have a big enough tank to make the trip, even if it says it is sorry or is really committed, that does not change the reality of the engine problem or the limited tank size.

So here is your diagnostic: *Look at the reality of the person.* Are they able to meet the demands of the reality that you are entrusting to them? Some of the most hopeless situations have lots of hope when the right person is brought in. Tough business situations get turned around when the right leader is brought to the tough reality. The question is, who are you trusting? Does the person already in place have the character, the gifts, the experience, or whatever is going to be required to make the future better? You can sometimes have hope for very difficult or unknown realities if you know that your hope is in the right person. Things may be stalled out, but if the right person is at the helm, you can still have hope. That is what great leaders do: negotiate tough times. This is a key question that boards have to deal with all the time. "Do we stick it out with current leadership even though things are not working?"

During a recent leadership consultation, I was working with an executive team on the topic of who you can trust and who you can't (see the next chapter). An executive raised his hand with this question:

"OK, I get it that there have to be reasons to move forward that are real and objective. But what about the person who somehow has that weird sixth sense to see things that no one else sees? They say we ought to go in a completely different direction, and it makes no objective sense, but they are right. There are people like that, you know. They come up with the idea that seems crazy, but it is the right one, and you should abandon everything that makes sense and go their way. It is irrational, but right. It happens all the time. Someone sees something that looks irrational to the rest of the herd, but they are *right*. There is no objective reason to believe it, but they are right."

"Great question," I said. "And one that actually makes my point. While they may have 'irrational' reasons for telling you to turn left when the whole world is turning right, it *can* be very rational for you to follow them. The reason all lies in one question: who is the person who is telling you to do the nutty thing? Is Steve Jobs saying, 'We can do a crazy thing that is exactly the opposite of what the rest of the world is doing—we can sell individual songs for ninety-nine cents each and be a computer business that goes into content distribution'? Hmmmm . . . . maybe someone should pay attention. Why? He is a proven innovator, someone who has the gifts, makeup, and experience to see a future that others don't see. So when he has an 'irrational idea,' we listen.

"But if the one who is telling you to do something irrational has aluminum foil on his head, then maybe not so much. It is not irrational to listen to a crazy idea from a proven sane performer. *It is often irrational to listen to a seemingly good idea from a proven nonperformer.* He may sound good, but his record may prove otherwise. If that is the case, we will stop listening to his thoughts."

Sometimes the one in place is the right one to have hope in for the future. You know what they are capable of, and just the fact that they are there is a hopeful objective reality. At other times, though, it is time for an ending, and someone new must be brought in for the hope to be more than a wish.

WHEN TO SUSPEND HOPELESSNESS

I have said above that the past is the best predictor of the future. But remember, I said that only applies if nothing changes or if *there is no rational reason to have hope.* One rational reason, then, is to have the right person in charge, whom we can trust to figure out the future and make a difference. Things turn around with the right people. So if you have that person in the situation, no matter how bleak, hopelessness may not be called for. Look what happened to

Apple when Jobs returned to leadership. Not so hopeless anymore.

Now for the harder question: Can I ever have hope when someone is currently failing but they are sorry and have a newfound commitment to doing better? When can I have hope for that? Do we always just throw someone away who is not doing well? Do we *always* have to create a necessary ending if there is a pattern of failure?

Absolutely not! People change. We can often have hope, as people do wake up and get it and change. But . . . not always. If you invest hope in their changing but they don't, you can waste more time, even years, and not get anything in return for your misplaced trust, other than more misery and more failure. So the question is this: when can I have hope that a person is going to be different in the future than he is now or in the past? Answer: again, look for the objective reasons to hope, other than their saying "I'm sorry" or "I am committed this time." You need a "reason to believe." Here are nine objective factors to help you determine whether you can have hope that tomorrow will be any different from today: verifiable involvement in a proven change process, additional structure, monitoring systems, new experience and skills, self-sustaining motivation, admission of need, the presence of support, skilled help, and some prior or current success.

Verifiable Involvement in a Proven Change Process

Is the person in some sort of change process that you can verify a sustained commitment to? For example, if an addict says that he is going to get sober, if we see him checking into rehab and staying the entire time, and if, after he is out, he goes to two AA meetings a day for a few months, stays in constant touch with his sponsor, goes to counseling, and so on, then there is a rational reason to have hope.

If a nonperformer in business commits to a change process of some sort, such as coaching or other verifiable, proven processes, that is a rational reason to suspend hopelessness. I recently worked with a corporate board that was in the process of selecting a new CEO. After much discussion, the board offered the job to a candidate who lacked experience in one critical area, but he agreed to get help from both a coach and outside consultants. The board had objective reasons to believe that the candidate recognized his limitations and was willing to undertake the necessary actions to fill this gap in experience. Because the candidate committed to a growth process, the board was able to offer him the job and feel that the future could be hopeful.

Additional Structure

By and large, people do not change without new structure. The change process must not be left up to the person's own schedule and internal controls. The process must include a structured path, i.e., set-in-stone times and practices that do not depend on the person's own whims, regular meetings with a coach, mentor, support group, trainer, or seminar.

Change must be structured for many reasons, but one is the way the brain works. Old patterns get reinforced unless a new discipline is introduced to override the old patterns. People who have never exercised on their own because of a lack of self-discipline cannot be trusted to all of a sudden begin to get in shape because the doctor says they need to. They usually need the structure of regular times with a trainer or a class in order to make the program sustainable. New brain patterns must be developed from outside structure. In business coaching, for example, I often require set, structured times when I and the executive or the team will be together, as opposed to just "when you have time or when you need it."

Monitoring Systems

How do we know this is all happening? Because we are watching it and measuring it. One company put together a subcommittee from the board of directors, which, like any other subcommittee, had a task: the development of the CEO. That committee regularly monitors the CEO's involvement in the process and his progress. It reports to the board of directors to show that the CEO is in compliance with the development program. They monitor the process. Why? Compliance with a change process is increased with monitoring. There is a reason that parents oversee little kids' homework times. With a lack of maturity or strengths, the natural drift is away from what is difficult and different, and monitoring is always essential to success.

New Experiences and Skills

People change not only because of new information, but also by gaining new experiences that teach them what they need in order to make the future different. In leadership coaching, for example, I am always attuned to what kinds of experiences a leader needs in order to actually internalize the change that he or she is looking to make. Then we design a path to gain those. Skills building can be a big part of that as well. I have sent many leaders to workshops, group experiences, off-sites, et cetera, knowing that the changes that were absolutely necessary to their success would never happen without such experiences. Information and insight are important to change, but experiences are crucial as well.

Self-sustaining Motivation

How do you know when to have hope for the future of someone's changes? *Look at the degree to which you are having to drive the process.* That is one of the strongest indicators of what is going to happen.

When people are on fire to change, they go to their meetings and their sessions without anyone making them. They do it on their own. They read books; they look for others in the change process; they seek experiences, listen to podcasts, and look for advice. You can just look at them and know that they have the fire to develop. As I write this, I am in a conference-center resort setting, as I usually have to get away from it all to work on a book. In this conference center, a convention is being held for people in direct-marketing sales organizations. I have run into several of them over the last few days, and you can instantly see their future. The fire that drove them here to learn how to make their businesses work, as well as the conversations I overhear in the restaurants and hallways, show their investment. No one is making them be here. They are here on their own dime and time. I love to see that kind of self-motivation and drive. I do not know if they would pass all of the other tests that we have mentioned, but in this one dimension, I would see hope for their future.

If you are hoping that someone is going to succeed in the future when the past has not been so great, look for this kind of hunger to make tomorrow different. If you are having to nag them into doing the work, chances are that if you quit nagging, then the work is going to stop as well. And if the work is not sustained, then the change is less likely to occur. Whenever I hear that an addict who got sober has stopped going to meetings, my heart sinks. It usually is a good predictor of a coming slide. The same is true of executives who get started in a coaching or development program but then get "too busy." Not a good sign for the future.

Admission of Need

To have hope that people are truly going to change, you must have an admission from them that they really *need* to change. They must see that they have a problem and own the problem.

Similarly, they must see that they have a need for help and that they cannot trust their own efforts to make anything different. Remember the analogy of the broken car: even if it is motivated, the engine is still broken and needs a mechanic. What you want to hear from someone is not only "I have a problem and need to change," but also "I need help and am looking for it." Taken together, these statements are hopeful, but one without the other is not. Someone who admits to a problem and is not getting help is stuck, and someone who is getting help but then always tries to convince the helper or the coach that she really doesn't have an issue is equally hopeless, at least for the time being. Change requires both.

The Presence of Support

In a change process, support is essential. Change takes place when we are surrounded by people who support our desire for change and growth, whether in our personal or our professional lives. Recent research has shown that a lot of what people desire in life, such as healthy lifestyles, is actually "contagious." If they are surrounded by overweight people, for example, they have a much higher chance of being overweight. But if they are surrounded by people who are healthy, that is contagious as well. Their efforts are supported and not thwarted.

In addition, those who are working toward change need people who are committed to their growth other than the assigned change agents or coaches. Besides the professional helpers, they need friends, family, or co-workers who are on their side and encourage them. That is a big force for change to reverse entropy. We need the energy of outside support to sustain an uphill battle. All successful systems of change involve a strong social-support component.

Conversely, if someone desires change but is still hanging around people who work against that change, the risk is much greater. An addict must, for example, lose the phone numbers of his addict friends. A nonperformer must shun other nonperformers. In the same ways that we worry about whom our kids hang around with, we need to worry about it in the change process for adults as well. This is another good reason to prune the nonperformers out of a company, as other people "catch" the sickness. And it is a good reason for leaders to make sure that the people they are trying to develop spend a lot of time around high-performers.

Skilled Help

Usually, for there to be real hope for the future, there must be someone in the circle of help who knows what he is doing. I have seen a lot of situations where someone is holding out hope for an executive or a loved one and they say, "It's going to be good. He's meeting with so-and-so." But so-and-so is not really bringing a lot to the table, and nothing changes. But at other times, I hear that they are meeting with a different so-and-so, and immediately I get hopeful because I know that "so-and-so number 2" is good.

I am all for peer-to-peer help, coaching, mentoring, and the like. It is usually an essential part of any change process. But the question is always What is that peer bringing to the party? The mere fact that someone has offered to help doesn't mean much. What matters is what kind of experience that person is bringing with them when they show up. How many such situations has she helped with before? What in his experience base would lead you to believe that he can help this person now? What kind of wisdom and knowledge does she offer?

In some situations, you just can't find the kind of help that would cause us to have much hope unless you tap professional know-how. Some situations require it, and in my experience, it is also good to make sure that you ask the professional how many such situations he or she has had experience in. A classic example of that is the mental health professional who is called to help an addict yet does not have much experience in treating addictions. In those instances, you want someone who has treated many addicts and knows all the tricks.

Executive coaching is similar. Depending on what kind of situation you find yourself needing help for, make sure that the coach has had experience in that kind of engagement, that size organization, or with that level of executive or team. Make sure that he is equipped to deal with someone like you or the one you are wanting to help. The bottom line is not someone's degrees or title, but her expertise and experience.

Some Success

Change takes time. One of the most common comments I hear from those who are invested in someone's changing is "I hope this happens fast." In some situations, we *can* expect enormous change in a short time with specific interventions. For example, I recently worked with a VP who had a horrible track record with direct reports. What I found was that he simply had never been taught how to talk to people in difficult conversations, and with a few months of coaching, he had turned around some key relationships. But in other kinds of situations, especially where long-standing personality issues are involved, change is a process. So, to have hope, you *must* have patience with people making significant changes.

But that does not mean that you should wait forever. There should be movement that can be seen, even if quite early in a process. Notice I did not say that you should see all of the *results* early on. What I said was "movement," as in progress. In other words, you should be able to ascertain that *something* is happening. It may even appear to be getting worse, as in some people change does go backward before it goes forward. But at least that is movement. Talk to the helper so as to understand what proper expectations are, and then look for those expected things to be occurring. Usually it is good not to have hope if nothing is happening for a long period of time. Something should be happening somewhere along the way, even if it is not the end result yet. We are looking for some sort of movement, instead of ongoing stagnation.

WHAT NEW WISDOM IS BEING ADDED?

Years ago, I began a chain of psychiatric hospital treatment programs and treatment centers with a business partner, Dr. John Townsend. At the time we began it, we were young clinicians who wanted to take our treatment methods and programs and scale them up. We knew that they were effective and proved, and we were confident that we could implement them on a larger scale. So we began a company.

All was going well on the treatment side, as probably could have been expected. But not too long into the venture, we were amassing a sizable operation in the nuts and bolts of a health care business. It was no longer a couple of clinicians admitting patients to their units and treating them. It was now complicated managed-care contract negotiations and significant deals with public companies that owned hospitals; we needed to move from a private-practice model, in which the phone rings at the office when someone needs treatment, to a professional call center that could take a call from the initial inquiry for help all the way through the insurance utilization process to admission. All of this was a lot different than we had first signed up for, a couple of excited, zealous "kids," if you will (I was twenty-nine), with a dream to help a bunch of people and build a sustainable business in the process.

As it grew and got more complicated, we began to get bogged down. In the beginning, the business was more clinically weighted than health-care-operations weighted. So our expertise was enough. But it did not take long until we were over our heads in many of those areas where we had no experience, like "capitated coverage" and other complicated insurance and health care management issues. I remember the "bogged down" moment clearly. We were at that point where we had built something sizable enough to have a weighty infrastructure, but not getting to critical mass fast enough to have it realize its full potential. The costs of the infrastructure were adding more and more pressure, but they were not yet producing the top-line revenues that would sustain the business in the long term. We needed more knowledge regarding those growth curves than we had between the two of us or with our other partners.

There were times when I was beginning to lose hope that our original vision for the business could be realized. The cash burn rate of the infrastructure was scary enough to have my attention, and the stall was enough to get us to a potential pruning moment. We needed a necessary ending to the approach we'd been trying or a reason to hope that was not a wish.

The moment came when we decided to bring in some seasoned health care operational professionals. We hired a consultant with years of experience in treatment center chains to do an audit of all of our operations and make some suggestions. The audit took a month, and his finding was "You guys need to hire someone like me." In other words, we needed expertise in the areas where we did not have it. He showed us that our focus on the clinical side was leaving a lot undone on the operations side of the equation. We needed someone from the industry to bring the wisdom we did not possess.

So we did just that. But we didn't hire someone like him. We hired *him*. He was surprised at our suggestion that he come aboard, but we talked him into it. We followed that move by hiring several other seasoned health care industry pros, who brought knowledge that we did not have and fleshed out the right team. To paraphrase Jim Collins, we finally got the right people on the bus in the right seats. From managed care to marketing to finance and media, we began to tap the knowledge base and build an organization much deeper in wisdom in those areas than we were.

It was not long before the entire picture began to take shape. All that we had built with our own experience and expertise—the critical mass of networks, providers, market share, reputation for good treatment, incredible doctors and psychologists on our team—began to gel and operate successfully because the expertise we had been missing was finally on board. In the next few years, we experienced great growth and profitability while succeeding in our primary mission of extending help to scores of people throughout the western United States in about forty markets. So the truth was that there had been hope, but we just could not see it at the time.

But why? Why was there hope and not just a wish? The reason that our stalled enterprise was able to gain steam was similar to a law of physics: entropy increases, or things get worse over time, *in a closed system.* But if you open the system up and bring in a new source of energy and a template or a structure of *truth* to give direction to the energy, things can turn around. Entropy can be reversed. That is what happened, *there was new truth to give direction to the energy that we were pouring into the enterprise.* The wisdom of the highly experienced health-care industry professionals gave us direction, structure, and a path. Everything reversed course and got better. They added what we did not have.

So the lesson here is this: you can have objective hope if you are bringing some new knowledge, wisdom, or know-how to the situation. Obviously if things are not working, you need a second opinion, some new ideas, some knowledge that is not present. Without that, you may only be wishing. But if you really are bringing new wisdom to bear on a situation that is hopeless, you might have good reason to have true, objective hope.

WHERE IS THE ENERGY FOR CHANGE?

In a situation where you have decided that you don't want more of the current or past performance and yet you don't know whether or not to have hope, the third diagnostic test is this: *where is the energy for change going to come from?*

If you have energy without intelligence, it will be wasted and not go toward a direction or a path. But likewise, intelligence or a plan without energy is not going anywhere at all. Even the best-laid plans will stagnate without a force driving them.

So the relevant diagnostic question regarding when to have hope is Where is the energy going to come from to change things? I have seen so many situations where there could be very real reasons for hope, where there is great wisdom, intelligence, and planning, but the energy component is under-resourced or not thought of at all. You need new infusions of energy toward the change process that you have decided upon.

You have to be able to answer the question Who is going to drive the change? Without a dedicated change agent, change usually does not happen. So to have hope that is not a wish, that question must be asked and the duty assigned.

Someone who has been on the change project part time may have to go for 100 percent focus on the change. It may mean that more bodies must be brought to the task. It may mean outside consultants to bring new energy to the team. It may mean that a team is put together with that assignment, like the committee I spoke of earlier, whose mission was the development of the leader. That is energy focused on change.

I like to suggest that organizations begin to build "powerful coalitions" of influence within and throughout the company, people who will own the change and drive it forward. You can do this with formal or informal structures, with matrix teams, or functional teams. The question is always Where is the force going to come from?

The same question applies to the personal arena as well. A common question I get is from women who want to get their husbands into "growth." They might have experienced personal growth themselves, and want it for them, or they want it for their marriages. "How do I get him to read books, or care about growing?" women often ask.

Usually the answer is *not* to leave the *How to Have an Intimate Marriage* book on the coffee table while he is on the couch watching ESPN, hoping that he is going to pick it up and read it. Instead, I like to suggest that the women stop trying to be the energy source themselves, and get their husbands in front of new sources of growth energy that he will open up his "system" to and be influenced by, namely, other men. The best way is for a wife to get her husband in a small couples group or retreat where there are other men who are talking about issues and growing. That will have a greater chance of getting him energized than waiting on him to be his own spark plug. This outside group can be a "powerful coalition" for change, a new source of energy to add to the mix.

Whether dealing with individuals, companies, or specific projects or strategies, if you don't have new energy, you will probably get more of what you were already getting. So ask yourself where that new juice is going to come from if you want to have real hope. Another question to ask is What will be the structure of the energy?

You can't just shoot "energy" at a problem without thinking through the correct "dosage." Energy infusion has a structure to it, described by a formula that includes the amount of energy needed plus the time intervals when it is needed. Think of your body. You have to have energy to run it, and that basically comes from your food. At certain intervals, you must infuse your body with a necessary amount of fuel that is related to your metabolism. Too little too seldom does not move you forward. Too much too often is unusable and turns to fat. The key is getting the right balance of time and amount—the right amount of calories and the right food groups infused at the right intervals. Translating this principle for the change that you are driving, you have to ask, What are the right amounts to give at each dose, and what are the right kinds of intervals for the infusion of energy? You want enough energy to get the change moving and to keep it moving until the next infusion of energy, yet not so much that everyone gets overfed and has to take a nap.

For example, I worked with a particularly high-performing business unit whose leader was renowned for driving hope and sustained movement in his troops. He did it through a daily, fifteen-minute morning meeting to cast vision, give information, share stories of success, and infuse strategy, thus giving a daily dose of energy that kept it all moving. He used these short meetings to make sure everyone was aligned around the goal, to catch problems early, and to give his team a space in which to share lessons and acknowledge progress. This daily infusion of energy kept the team and the process moving. It's worth noting that the meetings were short, and they didn't require preparation, so they weren't distractions from the real work of change; instead, they became moments to mark forward progress and even to celebrate those incremental steps in the right direction.

Looking at another realm entirely, the need to organize the energy is why addicts drying out are asked to go to ninety meetings in ninety days. The point is to get them going hard and get them going fast with a lot of energy into real hope for change. Similarly, football teams have twice-a-day practices to get change going right before the season. In my leadership coaching practice, the

structure of time and energy infusion varies, depending on what
we are trying to accomplish and whom I am dealing with. The
process ranges from face-to-face meetings every quarter with an
extended call once a month, to daylong or half-day meetings once
a month, to quarterly off-sites with teams and key players. There is
no "right" formula, other than what keeps things moving with the
right kinds of infusion to drive change. In a hospital, some people
are on a continuous IV drip, and others take a pill once a day. Some
can even be outpatients.

One of the best practitioners of this approach is Bill Hybels,
the founding pastor of one of the largest churches in America
and also one of the largest faith-based leadership movements in
the world, the Leadership Summit, which attracts faculty ranging
from former presidents to corporate titans. He does something he
calls the six-by-six. A six-by-six is the framework Hybels uses to
identify the six things he must "speak energy into over the next six
weeks." These six items may be projects, initiatives, tasks, people,
or whatever he is trying to drive, but he keeps the list right in front
of him on a three-by-five card and structures his time and energy
around it. "For the next six weeks speak energy into these six most
important agendas." That one little way of structuring energy
probably has something to do with why he and his team have accomplished so much over the years.

So the amount and the time vary: weekly meetings, quarterly
off-sites, daily reviews, all with different agendas, depending on
what you are trying to change. The point is to create a structure
that includes the right amount of energy and the right time intervals. *You need enough of a dose of energy to make it effective, and you need
the right interval of time so the effects are not lost before the next bit of energy is
injected.*

If you are applying this to your personal life, the same issue is in
play. If you have a therapist, meet frequently enough with enough

structure to maintain the energy for change. If you are trying to get in shape, use the buddy system or get a trainer who will inject energy at the right intervals into your change process. If you are trying to lose weight, a structured program is probably necessary to have hope where you have failed before. There is a reason that groups like Weight Watchers have regular meetings that you attend to keep the outside energy dose coming in. Remember, in your personal life, where you are trying to have hope for change in areas that have never changed before, outside energy infusions at the right, regular intervals with a structure to them is absolutely essential.

HOPE THAT DOES NOT DISAPPOINT

One of my favorite proverbs in this one: "Hope deferred makes the heart sick, but a longing fulfilled is a tree of life" (Proverbs 13:12, *New International Version Bible*). There are few sicknesses of the heart like hope deferred. Companies and individuals get sick and stall out when they keep hoping for something that just never happens.

In this chapter, we have examined some diagnostic questions for you to ask yourself, your team, or your organization about when to have hope and when to get to hopelessness. Necessary endings should come when there is real hopelessness, a real reason to think that something is in need of pruning. As we saw earlier, it is one of the best places that you can get to, because it will fuel change.

But many times people give up and have an "unnecessary ending," thinking that something is hopeless when it is *not*. What is needed is for their hope to be based on some real reasons to believe: persons with the skills to deal with the current lack of getting there, introduction of new knowledge about a path to get there, and sufficient energy to bring about change. To find out if something is hopeless or not, these are helpful diagnostics to consider.

But what if you are wondering whether or not to have an ending with a particular *person*? In your business or personal life, how can you know whether to keep going with a particular individual? Above, we outlined the path to change, but how do you know if you even should start on that path or not? How do you know when to keep trying with someone and when to give up and execute a necessary ending? That is the subject of our next chapter.

CHAPTER 7

The Wise, the Foolish, and the Evil: Identifying Which Kinds of People Deserve Your Trust

The time when you get to hopelessness can be one of the best moments for your future. To give up hope that something is going to change when it is not going to gets you unstuck immediately and brings energy. It brings life to the sickness of hope deferred.

And as we have seen, the decisions involving *people* can be some of the most difficult. We have talked about getting to the hopeless moment with people, and also how to design a process of change that actually has hope of being effective.

But how do you know if entering into that process of change with someone is even worth it? How do you know that it is going to help? Haven't you wondered that sometimes? "Are they ever going to change? Are they ever going to get better? Should I really keep working with them, thinking they are going to improve? Are my efforts to get them to change going to help anything at all?"

Or on the personal side of life, how do you know when to invest the effort with someone to work on making things better and when you should tell them that you are done talking about it? With whom do you try, and with whom do you say, "I'm done talking"? That is a question that, if properly answered, can save much time and heartache.

And it is the subject of this chapter: how to diagnose a person to know whether working on the issue is likely to help or not.

If you are a responsible and loving person, then *you might assume that other people are like you—responsible and loving.* They do the right thing, taking responsibility for themselves, for their mistakes, for their work. And they care about other people and how their actions affect those people. That is what you do, right? Right. You have concern about how what you do affects others. So doesn't it make sense that everyone else would be like you and really care? Sure, if you lived on Mars.

But this is planet Earth. And if you are going to succeed in life and business, you have to succeed on this planet, not Mars. The truth is that not everyone on planet Earth is like you. Not all take responsibility for themselves or care about how their actions are affecting other people or the mission. Moreover, some are even worse than that. Some people are actually out to do you harm.

If you do not accept this reality, then you are going to spend a lot of time wasting time, money, energy, love, resources, your heart, and everything else that matters to you on people who will either squander it or destroy it. That is why this chapter may be the most important one that you read. It is essential to understand that not everyone is going to be open or even desirous of the change that you are trying to bring about.

So how do we know who is trustworthy to continue investing time, energy, and resources in and who is not? How do we know when a necessary ending is required with a person?

We have no crystal balls, and as a result, any of us can get surprised. I have seen "rock solid, good characters," or so everyone thought, go south and ruin lives (although usually there were signs that no one saw). And I have seen absolute train wrecks turn around and become rock stars. So I would not claim that you can know for certain what anyone is going to do in the future. But . . .

Although predictions made from weather satellite data are not always right, they are right most of the time. They can see what is on the horizon and headed our way, though something still may change. And here is the good news: *there is a weather satellite for people, which will help you be right more than you are wrong.* And if you learn how to use it, you will save yourself untold grief, time, energy, money, and more.

The satellite that will give you the most accurate predictions is the ability to diagnose character. Once you learn the character traits that give real reason to hope that tomorrow can be different, you can know better whom you want to invite into your tomorrow. You can actually know that there is a real reason to go forward.

Likewise, once you know the traits that give zero reason for hope and in fact should help you get hopeless, you will know whom *not* to invite to your tomorrow, unless something changes. And as we will see, whether or not that change occurs probably depends more upon what *you* do than you realize. You have more influence to bring about change than you might think, but the key is knowing what to do with different kinds of people.

In this chapter, you are going to learn a simple way to diagnose character traits that lead to hope, as well as those that don't. And you are going to learn what to do with each type. Different types call for different strategies.

THE THREE KINDS OF PEOPLE

As a clinician, I hate simplistic, popularized, cheesy systems that people use to put others in boxes. Human behavior is much more complex than that, and when I hear those labels being tossed around, something in me wants to rebel and prove that particular system wrong. So here I go, doing something similar. But I would add that this way of seeing people is backed by a lot of clinical data and research, as well as by the experience of many, many people. These three categories are described by virtually every group that has ever studied human behavior. It is depicted in the great literature of the ages, and I bet it will ring true in your own experience with people as well. It will pass the sniff test, I assure you. So here we go.

There are basically three types of people in the world, or better, three styles of behavior that a person can exhibit in a particular time or context. There are many ways of describing these three categories, depending on whether you are a psychiatrist, an employer, a spouse, a lover, or a judge. They all use different words, but the same categories clearly emerge in people's behavior. I like the way that ancient wisdom literature puts it:

1. Wise people
2. Foolish people
3. Evil people

Those are the three categories of behavior that you will find yourself dealing with in virtually any situation involving others. Now here is the kicker: these three categories of people or behavior are very different in what motivates them and what sustains them. As a result, the ways to get them to change are very different as well. Therefore, here is what you have to realize:

You cannot deal with everyone in the same way.

Different people, in different categories, require different strategies. If you try to deal with a foolish person, for example, in the same way that you deal with a wise person, he will drive you crazy, and you will lose time, resources, and heart. And if you deal with an evil person at all, you might lose your business or your life. So it is essential that you understand very quickly whom you are dealing with and take the appropriate stances that will ensure that you create the necessary endings.

If you are bristling at such rigid categories, I understand. I do not mean them that way, either, as in reality they are not absolutely discrete. The reality is that most of us have some of all three in us. We can be wise in one situation or context or issue and not so much in another. But the reality is that when you see these behaviors in the people you are dealing with, you have to act accordingly and not worry about the label. These labels are not meant to be rigid, but helpful ways to identify particular patterns of behavior in people about whom you have to make tough decisions.

Which brings me back to my earlier point about the kind of person you are. Your problem may be that you deal with people in the same way that works for you. Here is what I mean: if you are a loving and responsible person, when there is a problem with your performance or when someone has an issue with you, you want somebody to come to you and tell you. You want people to let you know if there is something you can do better or if you are hurting them in some way.

And when they do that, what do you do? You listen, feel sorry about your performance or your treatment of them, and take ownership of your performance, results, or behavior. You observe yourself, you listen to their input, and you change. The outcome is that trust is built, the relationship is strengthened, and you have gotten better for the interaction. Therefore, you value input and see it as the way to deal with people.

And that's the problem. Because that works with you, that is what you naturally do with others when there is an issue or a problem or when things are not going the way you'd like them to go.

You address the problem, and you expect others to have the same kind of response when you are in their shoes: you expect them to own up and make a change.

That is a great plan, and you can expect everyone to do exactly that—on Mars. But on Earth, it does not always work, and that is why you cannot deal with all people in the same way. They are not all like you. What works with you will not work with everyone, and it is imperative that you figure out what kind of person you are trying to get to change. Otherwise, you will just assume that all are responsible people who will respond to your feedback. *And the ones who are not will cause you more and more trouble as you continue to give them feedback so they can change.* With them, you need a different strategy. So let's look now at the three kinds of people so that you will know what to do with each.

WISE PEOPLE

I was asked by the chairman of the board of a company I consult with to accompany him to a lunch with the CEO of their organization. So I could better understand what was going on, we met beforehand, and he told me of the concerns that he had with the newly placed leader. He said that he'd been chosen for his operational strengths, which were really needed in the environment at that time in this particular industry. It was a time to organize the chaos, set up new structures, and right the ship. He was perfect for that assignment.

But, the chairman said, he was concerned that the CEO did not seem like a visionary to him, and he knew that at some point, visionary leadership would be important. The operational crises would one day be over, and the company would then need someone to give it a longer-term vision and be able to get everyone on board to realize that vision. He did not see the new guy as being really able to do that. In fact, he had recently watched the CEO handle some current issues poorly, losing opportunities for internal mes-saging and communication of values, strategy, alignment, and the like. The chairman's concern was that he was operating well but not leading in the ways that would be required for the long run. So we came up with a list of issues to talk to him about at the lunch.

The challenge for the chairman was that he was still feeling the effects of working with the previous CEO, who had been very difficult to deal with in a lot of ways, particularly when it came to receiving feedback about his performance. As a result of that experience, the chariman had a lot of trepidation going into this lunch, fearing more of the same kinds of defensiveness and denial. He wanted me there to help structure the conversation, to serve as a facilitator or extra voice if needed, and probably to offer moral support in what could be a tough conversation. To say to a new CEO that you are concerned that he is not acting like a leader is a course fraught with potential land mines.

Depending on whom you are dealing with.

The chairman began by telling the CEO that he was glad to have the opportunity to talk to him in this setting, informally and not with the whole board, as he was going to have to say some things that might be difficult to hear and wanted to discuss them before they got to the level where board involvement might be necessary. At this point, it was just informal feedback to see what the CEO's thoughts were on some issues.

It was clear that the CEO could tell that this was not going to be a lot of happy talk. The tone of the lunch got a little more serious—not contentious, but the mood had clearly been set: we are here to talk about some important stuff, and it is not all good. The entrées were on their way, and I found myself wishing he had saved his prologue at least until after I had gotten to enjoy my lunch.

The chairman then went into a pretty awkward presentation of a list of ways he had noticed that the CEO was not acting "leaderly," as he put it. He named several instances in which he felt he was acting like a manager, not a leader, and said he thought that to make it as a CEO, he was going to have to do differently. If I had not known better, from the content list as he laid it out, I would have thought he was firing him. I braced myself for the response, putting myself in the CEO's shoes, thinking how difficult that feedback must have been to hear. (*Where is my entrée?* I remember thinking. *This could go bad.*)

What happened next literally caused my eyes to water. The CEO looked up, nodded slowly, and said, "You have just given a great list of the things that I need to learn how to do to be a great CEO. Those are definitely my opportunities to grow. I would like to get better in those areas. Can you guys help me?"

I don't exactly know how to describe it, as it was not a business response that was welling up inside of me. It was a human one. My heart was seeing, right in front of me, something that is good and pure about the best of people. The CEO heard frank feedback about himself and how he could do better, received it, and desired to make the effort to grow. Also, I think I was being moved by the very virtue we have been discussing: hope. I was seeing hope emerge before my very eyes. There is hope for people who are receptive to feedback and who take ownership of where they need to grow. This man would do fine. He would learn, and he would grow. And not only was I seeing hope for him, but also for the organization that he led. I saw good things in their future.

We went from there to talking about how the chairman and I, along with some leadership training, could be helpful to him. We came up with a structure for his development over the following year. He applied himself, and we found that he actually had the gifts and abilities to do what the chairman had been asking for, but he never had really seen those things done before and just needed a little coaching. He stepped up and did well. Now, years later, he is thriving in his role. Why? *He is wise.* And wise people learn from experience and make adjustments.

Wisdom certainly means many things. If you examine the various ways that wisdom has been discussed in philosophy, religion, and the behavioral sciences, they all involve a coming together of knowledge, understanding, insight, and discernment so that a person knows what is good and what to do. The bare definition can sometimes make the wise sound like the sage who knows it all, but another key ingredient of wisdom puts the others in perspective: *experience*. Wisdom comes from experience, either the experience of others or of oneself. And to let experience do its work, a person has to be open to receiving the lessons that it has to teach.

That is why I knew that the CEO would do fine. The person who ultimately does well is the one *who can learn from his own experience or the experience of others, make that learning a part of himself, and then deliver results from that experience base.* And that requires being open to feedback. This CEO was doing that. He was listening to feedback regarding his own experience, his performance, and where it was lacking, and he was gleaning insights from the experience of this seasoned chairman and a consultant. As a result, he would become better as he learned what he needed to do. He would use his natural strengths and gifts to implement what he was hearing, and he would do well. It was the wisdom of listening to feedback and learning from experience that ensured this.

Which brings us to the key diagnostic of the wise person:

When truth presents itself, the wise person sees the light, takes it in, and makes adjustments.

You have heard it said of people that they "saw the light." Wisdom is a stance that people take wherein they are open to hearing the truth, so when it comes, they listen to it and make the necessary changes to be aligned with that truth. Such people take feedback, correction, and training well. When you tell them something about their performance that is accurate, they hear it. They respond to it positively, and they apply it. You don't get resistance or a fight. In fact, they see it as a gift.

The result? They learn and they get better as a result of feedback. Wise people will always grow and get better, and as a result, when you are dealing with one, you have good reason to hope. If something is wrong, they can learn. They don't resist the truth that they have to align with. As the phrase goes, they "take it to heart." No defensiveness.

Now, there is something very important to realize here: *wise* does not mean smartest, brightest, most talented, most gifted, most charismatic, or charming. While wisdom may coexist with all of these traits, it is completely unrelated. It is very possible, as we shall see, to have brilliant, charming fools in your midst whom you or others have been fooled by precisely because they were so smart and gifted. More about that later. But for now, understand that this diagnostic is about one thing and one thing only: *a person's ability to take feedback and make the adjustment.* With people who can respond to feedback, given that they have the gifts and abilities that you need in your context, there is always hope.

The mature person meets the demands of life, while the immature person demands that life meet her demands. You can see how wisdom plays into maturity, as the wise person would take in the truth and adjust herself to meet whatever change truth is demanding of her. But without that ability, the demand would go unmet, and the person would remain unchanged as a result of the feedback, none the wiser. That is why the proverb says, "Correct a wise person and he will be wiser still." Feedback *helps* the wise. They value it.

Traits of Wise Persons

Here are some traits of the wise:

- When you give them feedback, they listen, take it in, and adjust their behavior accordingly.
- When you give them feedback, they embrace it positively. They say things like, "Thank you for telling me that. It helps me to know I come across that way. I didn't know that." Or "I really took what you said to heart, and here is what I did." Or "Thanks for caring enough to bring this to my attention. I needed to hear this." There is some sort of appreciation for the feedback, as they see it as something of value, even if it is hard to hear. You might hear them offer a response like, "Well, this was tough to hear, but it is good. It will help me even if it hurts."
- They own their performance, problems, and issues and take responsibility for them without excuses or blame.
- Your relationship is strengthened as a result of giving them feedback. They thank you for it, and see you as someone who cares enough about them to have a hard conversation. They experience you as being for their betterment.
- They empathize and express concern about the results of their behavior on others. If you tell them that something they are doing hurts you, you get a response that shows that it matters to them. "Wow, I didn't realize I had hurt you like that. I never would want to do that. I am sorry." Or they are concerned about how their performance is affecting the company or the team. "I am sad that I have been letting us down. I want to do better." Or "I will not let that happen again."

- They show remorse. You get a feeling that they have genuine concern about whatever the issue is and truly want to do better.
- In response to feedback, they go into future-oriented problem-solving mode. "I see this. How can I do better in the future?"
- They do not allow problems that have been addressed to turn into patterns. They change. They adjust and fix them. It does not mean that change will be instantaneous. There are few instant cures with no slips, as a goal is always being approximated until one gets there. That is why surgeons in training start on cadavers. But they listen and learn and eventually are wise enough to cut living people. Wise people likewise address their faults, and you see changes in actions and behaviors instead of patterns that go unaffected by the feedback.

Strategies for Dealing with a Wise Person

I have said that the pruning moment happens when we get to a good state of hopelessness, in which we know that more time is not going to help. An ending is needed because more time is not going to make that good bud the best bud, or the sick one get better, or bring the dead back to life. So what does knowing if you are dealing with a wise person have to do with hopelessness?

It tells you whether or not more time is justified in finding out if someone can get better. If you have a performance problem with a person or in some way he is not being the best, which you know is demanded for the position, then you have an important question: do I fix or do I replace? If you remember, that was Jack Welch's pruning command: "fix, close, or sell." Whether or not a person has the traits of wisdom will likely tell you if they will be fixable or not. You cannot fix people who will not take feedback, because from their perspective, they do not have a problem. So as far as they are concerned, there is nothing to fix. That is why they do not change.

But if a person can take feedback and coaching and use it, there is a real reason to have hope. It may not mean success is certain, as she could take it all to heart and still not have the gifts or abilities needed for the job. But then you would know for sure that more time would not help and your decision would be clear. Both of you have tried your best, and it just did not work. You gave help, she used your help, and still the fit was wrong. Move on down the road, and both of you can be happy.

Can you have hope that is not an empty wish with wise persons? Absolutely. Give them resources, train them, coach them. You will likely get a return on your investment. They will take it in and get better, and you will have avoided an unnecessary ending. If they do all of that and still are not up to the task, it will be clear that an ending truly is necessary, for both of you have done all you can.

The bottom line with a wise person is that *talking helps*. Feedback helps. They use it, so keep on talking until there is nothing left to discuss. In chapter 11, I will be giving some specific communication tips for having these and other kinds of sometimes difficult conversations. But for now, let's take a look at the next category of person.

THE FOOLISH PERSON

I witnessed the following conversation as my client was talking to his product manager.

"Kyle, I want to talk to you about the product launch. There were some issues, and I want us to figure out what happened," Tony, the boss, said.

"OK, let's do it. I got the numbers, and I know that it didn't get to where it was supposed to," Kyle replied.

"Right, what do you think happened?" Tony asked.

"Well, I think marketing just missed it. They had this whole emphasis for the local saturation, and I don't think that is where the real interest is," Kyle explained.

"I talked to them," my client said, "and they said that they were limited in the exposure they got because the coverage they wanted from the ads didn't happen. They said it conflicted with ads the television network had already sold before us."

"That could have happened, those guys at _____ network are idiots," Kyle said.

"What do you mean?" Tony asked.

"Well, they are so unorganized, they always screw it up."

"When I talked to media, they told me that the date had not been reserved for our ads because your final graphics hadn't been sent in time, and they said they had asked you for them weeks before and never got a reply—even after several requests," Tony said.

"I doubt that's true, but it could be. IT has lost a lot of e-mail lately, and it is possible that I never got it," he said.

"But that isn't what concerns me," said Tony. "This is not about IT or the network or e-mail. The launch is *your* deal. If it works, it is because you made it work, and if the TV network was not cued up to go in time, it seems like you would have been monitoring this to know that we had a problem. Then, even if it *were* IT, you would have known it and been on top of it. As a result, we have really missed our number, and it is going to affect a lot. I need better than this."

"But I can't control the network. I made sure that media had put in the buy, and they should have known that it was not all nailed down. They should have seen this," he retorted.

"Kyle," the boss said, "media reports to you in this chain. This is yours."

"Yeah, but I did my part with them. If the galleys weren't there,

I had given them the time schedules, and they should have caught it," he explained. "Besides, that was the week that you pulled me over to work on next year's catalogue. I wasn't even here to be aware of what they were doing."

At this point, I interrupted the conversation. I turned to Tony and asked him a very simple question: "Tony, how are you feeling about this?"

Tony sighed and said one word: "Hopeless."

"I can see why," I said. "Seems like the problem is never here in the room."

And that is the problem with the fool. Whereas the chief descriptor of the wise person is that when the light shows up, he looks at it, receives it, joins it, and adjusts his behavior to align with the light, the fool does the opposite: *he rejects the feedback, resists it, explains it away, and does nothing to adjust to meet its requirements.* In short,

---

The fool tries to adjust the truth so he does not have to adjust to it.

We saw how the wise person adjusts to the truth. In contrast, the fool adjusts the truth so he has to do nothing different. He is never wrong; someone else is. If you have had the above conversation, which I am sure you have had with the Kyles in your own work or life, you know exactly what Tony was feeling: hopeless. The reason is that Kyle was taking no ownership of the problem. Giving feedback was hopeless. Therefore, as we shall see, *it makes no sense to keep giving it,* but more about that in a moment.

You probably know this experience. It is the gnawing feeling that you get when you have the same conversation with someone about the same issue over and over, and slowly sink into the frustration and despair of hope deferred. You wish that the person would hear what you are saying, as your intent is not to persecute but to solve a problem so that something will work or that your relationship will get better. But you get nowhere and mostly feel stuck. You try over and over, and yet nothing ever happens.

The point to understand here is that that is exactly what someone engaged in the foolishness of defending against seeing the truth is trying to accomplish. She is in a stance that is designed not to see the truth or grasp it or in any way adjust to it. Her goal is to avoid ownership of the feedback, which would require her to take responsibility and change. As a result, she constantly produces collateral damage for others, does harm to the cause, and everyone but her feels the effects. So, the frustration all around her grows.

Just as *wise* does not necessarily mean smart or extremely gifted, *foolish* does not mean dumb or lacking talent. Ironically, a fool actually may be "the smartest person in the room," or the most gifted or charming. Because of that, fools often keep us confused because of their many wonderful attributes. Our attraction to their talents and gifts keeps us hooked and makes it difficult to give up on them. So we continue to try, thinking that "one more conversation" will do the trick. But we get more of the same kind of behavior each time we try to solve a problem or give input, coaching, or correction.

Traits of Foolish Persons
- When given feedback, they are defensive and immediately come back at you with a reason why it is not their fault.
- When a mistake is pointed out, they externalize the mistake and blame someone else.
- Unlike the wise person, with whom talking through issues strengthens your relationship, with the foolish person, attempts to talk about problems create conflict, alienation, or a breach in the relationship.

- Sometimes, they immediately shift the blame to you, as they "shoot the messenger" and make it somehow your fault. "Well, if you had given me more resources, I could have gotten it done. But you cut my budget." Or "That's because you told me to make sure that I focused on the other project." Or "You never told me that you wanted it that way." The energy shifts, and suddenly you find yourself the object of correction.

- They often use minimization, trying to in some way convince you that "It's not that bad" or "This really isn't the problem that you think it is. It's not that big a deal."

- They rationalize, giving reasons why their performance was certainly understandable.

- Excuses are rampant, and they never take ownership of the issue.

- Their emotional response has nothing to do with remorse; instead they get angry at you for being on their case, attacking with such lines as "You never think I do anything right," or "How could you bring this up after all I have done?" Or they go into the "all bad" position, saying something like "I guess I can't do anything right," which is a cue for you to rescue them and point out how good they really are.

- They begin their response with "Well, you . . ." and get you off-topic by pointing out your flaws.

- They have little or no awareness or concern for the pain or frustration that they are causing others or the mission. While their behavior or performance creates a lot of collateral damage for others, they seem oblivious to it and see others as the problem for thinking that there is an issue.

- Their emotional stance toward getting corrected is opposite to that of the wise person, who embraces the feedback and shows appreciation for your taking the effort to share it. Instead, their stance is one of anger, disdain, or some other fight-or-flight response. They either move against you or move away from you as a result. I have heard many people say that after they confronted someone with something, the person never talked to them again if they did not have to.

- They see themselves as the victim, and they see the people who confront them as persecutors for pointing out the problem. They feel like the morally superior victim and often find someone to rescue them and agree with how bad you are for being "against" them.

- Their world is divided into the good guys and the bad guys. The good ones are the ones who agree with them and see them as good, and the bad ones are the ones who don't think that they are perfect.

The important theme to recognize in all of these traits is a lack of ownership of the issue and a refusal to take responsibility and change behavior to meet the demands of life. Instead, fools want reality to change for them. They always want the outside world to change instead of them.

Strategies for Dealing with the Foolish Person

We began with the problem that loving and responsible people have—they assume that everyone is like them and will respond to feedback. They think that if they just point out a problem to someone, the other person will respond as they do and take responsibility and change. But, as we have just seen, foolish people are not like them at all. In fact, they are exactly the opposite, desiring to *not change and not listen.* Which brings us to the strategic issue: Whereas talking about a problem to a responsible, wise person helps, talking about a problem with a fool *does not help at all. Therefore, further talking about problems is not the answer.*

So stop talking.

At least about the problem. Remember the definition of *crazy*—continuing to do the same thing expecting different results. If you have had this conversation sixty-three times, do you really think that number sixty-four is going to do the magic? The not-so-technical word for this is *nagging.* Nagging or any other kind of repeated attempts to get someone to listen should never have to be done, and if you are having to do it, something is wrong. After repeated attempts to get him to see an issue, *it is time to quit talking about the problem and time to have a different kind of conversation.* Stop talking about the problems, and talk about a new problem: *the new problem to talk about is that talking doesn't help.*

At this point, it is time to change the conversation from trying to get them to change to talking about the fact that no change is happening and that is the problem.

"Joe, I have talked to you about *a, b,* or *c* on several occasions, and I do not want to talk about those anymore. It is not helping. What I want to talk about now is a different problem. The problem that I want to talk about is that trying to talk to you about a problem does not help. So what would you suggest we do about that? How can I give you feedback so that you will listen to it and do something about it?"

Sometimes this may get a response, and if it does, you are a step farther down the road. But chances are that you will get more of the same, and at that point, it is time to go to the strategy of creating a necessary ending of this pattern. The way you do that is by no longer having conversations about the problem, but rather by setting limits on the problem instead of trying to solve it through talking about it. While the strategy with a wise person was to talk about problems and resource them with more input and help, the strategy with a foolish person is to stop talking and move to two important interventions: *limits* and *consequences*.

First of all, set limits on yourself in terms of what you will allow yourself to be exposed to in terms of the fool's collateral damage:

- "Susie, at this point, I have tried to get you to see the issue and change it, and that has not helped. So I have to make sure that at least it is not affecting me [or the team, or the company, or the results, or the family] any more. I can't afford to miss another quarter's numbers because you are unwilling to do what I have asked. So I am taking this responsibility away from you. I have to give it to someone who will do what I need."
- "Sam, I cannot allow myself to continue to be hurt or endangered by your drinking. So the next time it happens, I will leave the event or the house and go somewhere where I am not affected by it."
- "Keith, your anger is hurtful to me, and I can't allow myself to be yelled at anymore, so the next time it happens, I will leave."
- "Roger, this team and the environment we want to have around here are important to me, so I can't allow your abusive behavior to ruin it anymore."

Consequences are often the next essential step. Whereas feedback has not helped and limits will protect you from the collateral damage of someone who avoids ownership, consequences are the last step that may cause the person to hit bottom and "see the light." Consequences are for their sake, perhaps to get them to turn things around:

- "Mary, we have had several gatherings where you have drunk too much and ruined it for everyone, so I need to tell you that until you can control yourself, we won't be including you anymore. You are no longer invited."
- "Bill, we have had several discussions about your performance, and nothing is changing, so I am going to have to remove you from your position."
- "Roger, we have talked about this a number of times, and I have tried to get some changes from you, but it is not working. I am giving you an unpaid suspension to think about it and see if you would like to continue here and under what circumstances that might happen."
- "Dave, I want to live in a sober house, and since you have chosen to not do anything about your addiction, I won't be living with you anymore until you get treatment and get sober."
- "Barbara, I wish that I could continue to have you as a client, but I have talked to you about the problems that make this difficult for me. Since you have chosen to not change those issues, I can no longer do work for you. If something changes, feel free to let me know."

The strategy for foolish people is simple: Quit talking about the problem and clearly communicate that because talking is not helping, you are going to take steps to protect what is important to you, the mission, or other people. Give limits that stop the collateral damage of their refusal to change, and where appropriate, give consequences that will cause them to feel the pain of their choice to not listen.

The necessary ending that you have to initiate with people caught in their own foolishness is to *end the pattern*. You cannot control them or get them to change. What you can do is *create an ending to the effects their refusal to take responsibility is having on you or others*. By so doing, you have accomplished two things that nagging did not do. You have limited the effects of their behavior on you and others, thus quarantining their ownership disease from further infecting your life, the team, or the mission, *and you may have done the one thing that can influence them to change. Talking will not help, but doing something that causes them to feel the consequences of their behavior may be what finally turns them around.*

The key here is to see that holding out hope for someone who is resistant to feedback is not grounded in a lot of reality. It is hard enough to fix some problems when someone owns them. But if they are in denial about them, then they are not even working on them, and there is not much reason to have hope until they do. *This is why it is so important for you to recognize foolish behavior.* Once you see it, you know that an ending is nigh—if not an ending with the person, then at least an end to allowing their unchanging pattern to affect you or things you care about. Otherwise, you cannot have hope that tomorrow is going to be different from today.

The Key to Changing a Foolish Person's Behavior

As we have seen, there is a big difference between ending a wise person's problem behavior and ending a foolish person's. With the wise, if you talk about it, resource them, and help them, you usually get improvement. With the foolish, talking usually does nothing, and only consequences matter. Let's talk about that for a moment, so you see how essential this point is and why you sometimes have to bring consequences into the picture.

Whenever someone is not taking responsibility, there are always consequences. The question is, Who is *suffering* the consequences? Most times, with someone who is not responsive to feedback, their

company, team, boss, co-workers, or loved ones are the ones who
are suffering the consequences of their behavior. An addict, for
example, is not trying to ruin anyone's life; he is just trying to avoid
responsibility for his problems. But as a result of not taking responsibility, he ruins many people's lives with the "collateral damage" of
his addiction. There are certainly consequences, but he is not the
one who is suffering them. Others are.

On the job, when someone is not owning her issues, it is usually the company, the team, or co-workers who are suffering the
consequences—a toxic culture, being held up, not meeting deadlines, not getting deals done, losing potential profits, losing customers, not accomplishing the mission, et cetera. They are suffering, as
they are all working hard, taking responsibility for themselves, and
yet paying for the results of her denial.

So as long as you are not creating a necessary ending to this
pattern, there is no force driving change, because the person has
no consequences. *With these kinds of people, the only time they get it is when
it begins to cost them.* That is the only time they feel any need to listen
and change. It is exactly why a necessary ending is often the right
thing to do.

I frequently hear bosses, co-workers, and others say to a person
in this kind of denial, "You *need* to begin getting your reports in on
time so we can move forward and hit our deadlines." Then they say
to me, "I told him he needs to do it, but he still doesn't."

I usually say it is not true that he needs to do it. "Apparently
he does not need to at all, or he would be doing it. It sounds as
though *you* need him to do it and that *you* are the only one who feels
the need for him to perform. He obviously feels no need at all. I
think what we have to talk about is how to *transfer the need for him to
perform from your shoulders onto his, as he is the only person who can do anything about it.*" Consequences are the way to do that. When people
begin to feel consequences for their behavior or performance, all of

a sudden they realize that "I need to perform, or I am going to get fired." The need has finally been transferred from the shoulders of the people who should not be experiencing it to the shoulders of the one who should.

When a spouse says to the alcoholic, "You need to go to AA," that is obviously not true. The addict feels no need to do that at all, and isn't. But when she says, "I am moving out and will be open to getting back together when you are getting treatment for your addiction," then all of a sudden the addict feels "*I need* to get some help or I am going to lose my marriage." The need has been transferred. It is the same with any kind of problematic behavior of a person who is not taking feedback and ownership. The need and drive to do something about it must be transferred to that person, and that is done through having consequences that finally make him feel the pain instead of others. When he feels the pain, he will feel the need to change.

So, in terms of when to have hope and when not to, if you are hoping that someone in denial is going to get it and change, but there is nothing in the picture to force that change other than your desire, that is probably a wish and not real, objective hope. If you are dealing with this kind of person, it is probably time for a necessary ending to the pattern of not listening and the beginning of a different plan. A plan that has hope is one that limits your exposure to the foolish person's issues and forces him to feel the consequences of his performance so that he might have hope of waking up and changing.

EVIL PEOPLE

Sometimes in a workshop or in leadership training, in teaching about these three categories of people, I will summarize the methods of dealing with them like this in order to introduce the concept of the evil person:

1. With wise people, talk to them, give them resources, and you will get a return.
2. With foolish people, stop talking to them about problems; they are not listening. And stop supplying resources; they squander them. Instead, give them limits and consequences.
3. With evil people, to quote a Warren Zevon song, the strategy is "Lawyers, Guns and Money." The reason? You have to go into protection mode, not helping mode, when dealing with evil people.

Lawyers, guns, and money usually get their attention. That introduction is not only for effect. The truth is that I am not kidding.

Lawyers, Guns, and Money: A Tough Pill to Swallow

For some people, it is a big step to realize that there are people in the world who hurt you—not unintentionally the way a foolish person does but because they *want to*. But it is true. There are some people whose desire it is to hurt others and do destructive things. And with them, you have to protect yourself, your company, your loved ones, and anything that matters to you. They actually want to bring you down.

This is difficult for some leaders to come to grips with; they think that they can reason with anyone and finally get through. But evil people are not reasonable. They seek to destroy. So you have to protect yourself—ergo, lawyers, guns, and money.

I use that phrase to symbolize resources that you use to protect yourself. Sometimes you must see people for who they truly are, protect yourself, create a *very* necessary ending, and have nothing more to do with them. The kind of person who likes to bring others down, is intentionally divisive, enjoys it when someone fails, and tries to create the downfall of others or of the company is to be protected against at all costs. The longer that you have hope for this kind of person, the more vulnerable you are.

Many women have to get restraining orders, as they are in relationships with destructive men and their very lives are in danger. They need to create a very firm, necessary ending with no contact and be protected by their attorneys, police, and others: ergo, lawyers, guns (police), and money.

But this is true in business, as well. Rarely is there physical danger; more often it is an individual's career or the company that is in danger. There are people who do want to bring you down and destroy whatever you have built—for many reasons. They envy you and want your position, or they think they were slighted and want to sue you to get back at you. I have seen some ugly things happen in the business world, and some of it could have been avoided if people had not held out false hope for dealing with a person who engaged in a lot of evil behavior. Do not hope for the evil persons to change. It could happen, and it does, *but it does not happen by giving in to them, reasoning with them, or giving them another chance to hurt you*. It happens when they finally are subject to limits that force them to change. Jail does some people good.

The bottom line with evil is to stay away, create the firmest protective ending that you can, and get real help to do it. Use your lawyers, law enforcement (that is the guns part), and your financial resources to make sure that you will not be hurt by someone who is trying to destroy you or the things that matter to you. Whereas you talk to wise people about problems and you talk to fools about consequences, do not talk to evil people at all, period. "You can communicate with me through my attorney" is a phrase that exists for a reason.

Problems versus Patterns

Another thing to consider when you are trying to figure out if you are going to go forward with a person is the issue of problems versus patterns. A problem is something in someone's performance or behavior that you need to end; it is specific and objective and isolated. For example, a big project is blown because of a specific mistake or because an interpersonal conflict is not handled well.

A pattern exists when there are problems but they do not stand alone as isolated issues or occurrences. Instead, you can link many occurrences together to see that this person made a mistake on the big project because she didn't get organized or do her research. And this is just one more example of many times when she has done the same or similar things. It is not a specific, one-time problem. It is a pattern that we can recognize and now almost count on. It is recurring.

When you are dealing with a recurring pattern, there is less hope that just a conversation or a little correction is going to help. Patterns, many times (though not all), are tendencies that people have less conscious control over, and the process of change is more difficult. Change certainly can happen, but if you are depending on it in any significant way and need to have hope for long-standing patterns to change, then look at the ingredients of the change process that I listed in Chapter 6 in the section entitled "When to Suspend Hopelessness."

Hope and the Strengths Movement

One of the great emphases of recent management literature has been the strengths movement. Championed by the Gallup Organization, organizational researcher Marcus Buckingham, and others, the message is a good one: people do better when operating from their strengths than from their weaknesses, and companies do better when they are making sure that people spend their time and energy doing what they are good at rather than what they are not.

This finding is relevant to our discussion about hope in two ways. The first is that sometimes a person's performance is not going to get better if you continue to have her doing something for which she has very little giftedness, ability, or inclination. You are swimming upstream to try to hold on to the hope that it is going to get better. A better move is to see what happens if you move that person to an area that uses her strengths. Then you might have a lot more hope for better performance.

This is true in personal life, as well. I have seen marriages turn around when a long-standing conflict over one spouse's nonperformance gets reversed because the couple decides to change roles in that area. I remember one marriage in which the wife was continually disappointed in her husband's handling of the finances, an area that he had zero inclination for but that both of them thought was "the man's role" in the family. She was much more organized, better at dealing with numbers, time lines, details, and so on, and she actually enjoyed it. So they got over their thinking that the man should handle the money, turned it over to her, gave him some of the other responsibilities that she was carrying, and they did very well. Strengths matter, so base some of your hope on them.

There is another way strengths matter when it comes to hope: sometimes people are indeed operating in their area of strength, but their character issues are so formidable that their strengths are neutralized. They may be very creative but so disorganized and such procrastinators that you can't get a project done. Or so combative that they can't be a member of a team. In those cases, it is not a matter of getting them to focus on their strengths, as they already are. It is a matter of seeing if they will deal with their basic character problems, in the manner we talked about in the last chapter. If they will, there is hope. If they won't, then looking for other areas of gifts may not matter. There is a difference between *strengths* and *character*. See my book *Integrity: The Courage to Meet the Demands of Reality* (HarperCollins, 2006) for more on this issue.

It's All About Hope

Necessary endings happen when you get to a "good hopelessness." It is that moment when you see reality clearly and know you have to bring "what is" to an end. Unfortunately, sometimes that decision involves people, and deciding when to keep going with someone and when not to is one of the most difficult decisions that we have to make, and we must make it in many contexts, throughout life. It was much of what Peter Drucker referred to as the "life and death decisions" for leaders, and it is true in the personal space as well.

So making people decisions should never be taken lightly. It is crucial that we have good criteria for when to have hope and when to reach hopelessness. If you have hope in someone who is in denial, that is usually misspent time, energy, and resources. At the same time, as we have seen, there can be hope for them if you do the right thing and create an ending, that is, stop enabling the pattern by implementing some limits and consequences.

Conversely, other people can readily change, given the right input, because they are wise and open to hearing what you have to say. There can be great hope in many instances, provided they have the gifts and abilities to deliver what you want from them.

Seeing the differences between wise, foolish, and evil people will be a good tool for you in making those difficult decisions.

CHAPTER 8

Creating Urgency: Stay Motivated and Energized for Change

I know I live in hell, but I know the names of all the streets." This is exactly the response one woman made to a group of friends who were trying to get her to take some positive steps in her life. I will never forget her words, as they epitomize one of the biggest problems in creating necessary endings in all of our lives. Endings, no matter how needed, are hard. They involve change, and for many reasons that we have seen, we resist the changes that we need to make, even when they would be good for us personally or for our business.

Your brain's hard wiring can resist change, as we have seen. But at the same time, you know you must change if you are going to end the misery of the present and get to the future that you desire. Both the resistance and the imperative are real, and both require attention.

We have examined some of the personal maps and belief systems that may have slowed you down. What we will do now is look at some of the *accelerators* that will get you moving, and some of *the in-the-*

moment thinking patterns that slow you down and keep you from making the changes you need to make. In essence, this chapter is about two forces: time and energy. Time is working either for you or against you in terms of your needed ending. If you are stalling or waiting, then you are tacitly agreeing to more of what you already have or worse. If you are not creating urgent energy toward an ending, you will have no movement. So to get past the inertia of the past and present, you need to do both: address the urgency and the stall.

CREATING URGENCY

You have heard it said that people resist change. That is not always true. It is more true that people resist change that they feel no real need to make. For example, if I said, "Get up and go outside," but you were relatively comfortable where you are, you would resist my suggestion. But if I said, "The building is on fire! Get out now!" we would see little resistance to change. We will quickly make changes that we feel will make pain stop or help us avoid it.

On the positive side, we will do the same thing. If I asked you to stop shopping where you shop but you were pretty comfortable at your present store, then you would not go out of your way to change. But if I told you that another store, even a few miles farther down the road was offering three for one, you would be more likely to go. So getting your brain to move to create an ending, and getting the people around you to do the same, *is going to take both: the fear of the negative and the draw of the positive.* Your brain needs to really get it—that if you don't move, something bad is going to happen, and also that if you do, you will get what you desire. You have to break through the comfort level that you are in, where you are settling for living in hell just because you know the names of all the streets. Remember, *you were not designed to cope but to thrive.* But just like a rosebush, you can't thrive without pruning, which means your necessary endings truly are urgent. Let's look at how to get there.

STRATEGIES FOR CREATING URGENCY

We saw how previous experience had seared urgency into the brain of one CEO, Julie Shimer. All she had to do was to replay that movie in her present situation and she heard "fire alarms" going off all over the place. She immediately felt the urgency and made courageous moves.

Playing the movie forward is one of the best known motivators in human behavior, as it gets your brain aligned with what you want and can create new patterns of behavior. Remember, we saw how your brain will get you moving toward anything that it agrees with, and avoiding pain is tops on its list. The usual problem with "living in hell but knowing the names of all the streets" is that you are not in enough current pain to create urgency. We get comfortable with our misery, as we find ways to medicate ourselves, delude ourselves, disassociate our feelings, or get enough distance from the problem that it does not touch us directly. CEOs and other leaders, for example, can often stay far enough "above" the real problems in the trenches that they do not feel the urgency to change. Remember Shimer's description of how Motorola people were able to stay away from the painful pending reality by consoling themselves with the belief that their market share would save them from the digital revolution. We all use similar tricks, as we shall see later in this chapter.

So, the first step to getting to the necessary ending that we need is to *make the threat to our future as real in our minds as it is in reality.* That means that we have to smell the smoke. Most change experts talk about the need to "see the future" that awaits, clearly and vividly, in order to get movement out of our comfort zones. Here is how change expert John Kotter describes it in *A Sense of Urgency* (Boston: Harvard Business Press, 2008):

> *Urgent behavior is not driven by a belief that all is well or that every-*
> *thing is a mess, but, instead, that the world contains* great opportuni-
> ties and great hazards *[emphasis added]. Even so, urgent action is not*

created by feelings of contentment, anxiety, frustration, or anger, but by a
gut-level determination to move, and win, now. These feelings quite natu-
rally lead to behavior in which people are alert and proactive, in which
they constantly scan the environment around them, both inside and out-
side their organizations, looking for information relevant to success and
survival. With complacency or false urgency, people look inward, not out,
and they miss what is essential for prosperity.

This is a great description of how feelings that are truly motivating have to be related to reality, as opposed to a numb complacency medicated by all sorts of excuses, or to an emotional crisis
created by a nagging or angry boss or spouse. The ones that work
come from within, from seeing the world as it really is, motivated
by its dangers and opportunities. This is why interventions with
addicts work when nagging doesn't, and why real P&Ls have an
effect on boards and executives that words don't. Earnings reports
create action in boardrooms. Reality can move us. In my view, that
is why Kotter's suggestion to get people to go outside of the organization helps, as they begin to "open the system" and infuse it with
the truth of the real opportunities and storms brewing outside the
walls of the company.

So, back to our question. How do you make the brain smell the
smoke? How do you get the heart to align with the needed change?
My suggestion is to "play the movie": "Do you want to look the
way you do now, overweight, in June, on the beach?" Or "Do you
want to still be losing market share this time next year because you
haven't fired your VP of sales?" Make your heart and mind feel the
reality today that is surely coming tomorrow. And remember, both
the hazards and the opportunities must be felt.

Here is how. Get alone and get honest with yourself. Look in
the mirror if you have to, and ask that person if he or she wants
you to lie to you or tell the truth. If the answer came back "Lie,"

then you can stop reading this book. If you lie to yourself, you will never get there. But if the answer was "Tell the truth," then sit down and think of all of the realities of the situation that you have been avoiding:

- The continued frustration with a particular person's performance
- The continued frustration with the difficulties of trying to get someone to hear something
- The continued frustration of poor returns
- The continued frustration in a relationship
- The continued frustration of a pattern of yours or someone else's
- The continued frustration of a particular business line or strategy not working

Then, stop the excusing, the medicating, the rationalizing, or any other interference, and project into the future: one month, six months, one year, two years, five years, or more. See yourself at that time having the same discussions that you are having now, with no better results. Picture it, feel it, smell it. You already know what it is like, so you don't even have to use your imagination. You are living it right now. I just want you to picture yourself living it for real five years from now. Is that what you want?

I had an employee once whom I really liked working with in many ways. He had many strengths. But he continued to make the same mistakes over and over, and after many, many conversations to get him to improve and his not seeing a need to make any changes, I got hopeless and finally made a change. I had resisted for a long time because of all of his strengths, as I really wanted him to make it. This kept me stuck for a while.

But one day it all changed. I pictured myself dealing with these same issues a year from then, and I got sick to my stomach. In the day-to-day, I was able to numb myself to it, hoping for change and trying to ignore some things. But the reality was that I was sick of dealing with the poor performance in the areas where it was poor, and what put me over the edge was *seeing that the future was going to be just like today.* I wanted better than that for myself and my team, and "playing the movie forward" was all it took.

The reason was that my brain got aligned. I showed it a fire ahead, and it finally said, "I don't want to go there. I will make a change." Until then, I had been trying to motivate it to take some uncomfortable steps in a firing, but it could resist because there was no bigger pain looming. But when I played the movie forward, my whole being finally got aligned with action and said, "OK, there is no way I want to be doing this in another year."

One woman told me that this method is what finally got her to step up and end a six-year relationship with a boyfriend. She said that she had gotten comfortable with the lack of emotional intimacy in the day-to-day, always feeling as though she could put up with it *today* because of other reasons. She had kind of numbed herself to it. Then, one day, she said that she looked into the future and saw herself married to him, feeling alone in her marriage, and something snapped inside. She knew that she had to end it, so she did. Today she is in a better relationship.

Fortunately, she was single, and that kind of ending is part of the path in most people's journey. But even in the covenant of marriage, which is designed not to end, there should still be endings to unfulfilling patterns, and playing the movie forward is what finally gets people to stand up and say, "I do not want to be feeling this way about us for the rest of our lives. We have to get some help." Or "I don't want to be living with your addiction this time next year, or even next month. Get treatment or move out."

We have an incredible tolerance for pain, especially if we think it "might get better." So, we tell ourselves little lies like "It will turn around" or "It's not always like this." So we make it through the day, and another, until the days turn into years. But the truth is that there is no ending or better time coming unless we do something. So we have to get our mind to see that "hazard," as Kotter terms it, and stop the lies.

Recently a friend told me how he quit smoking. He got a coach who made him play the movie forward to feel the future reality of his habit where his heart would feel it: with his kids. He has two little boys, five and seven. So all his coach did was tell him that he had to take their photos and put them inside the cellophane wrapper of his cigarette package. That way, every time he took out a cigarette, he had to look at the photos of his little boys first, and picture them fatherless when he dies a premature death. That is a lot different and a more powerful approach than simply nagging someone with "You should quit smoking."

The reason is that it creates a painful reality that he would move to avoid, instead of a merely uncomfortable reality that he would avoid, i.e., nicotine withdrawal. Quitting gets uncomfortable, and most people avoid that discomfort—unless they are staring into the faces of their children at that moment. Then it brings the ability to create the ending. It is the same reason that interventions work with addicts when you can get all of the loved ones in a room sharing the pain that the addiction has caused them and giving the absolute promise that they are leaving if he doesn't go right into treatment. In the good interventions, the group also expresses a vision of the great opportunities that lie ahead if the addict gets treatment: we will all be together and be a family.

Whether in a business or a life, bringing the future misery into a very real experience today will create urgency. Sometimes that future misery is in continued frustration, and sometimes it is in future loss and regret that you will have if an ending does not occur. I talked to one leader once about his pattern of disconnecting from his junior high school–age daughter and asked him to think hard about the time when she'd be leaving for college and the risk of not knowing her. What would that loss and regret feel like? Playing that movie of future loss was what got him to change.

And the technique works not just on the negative side, but the positive side as well. What helped me pull the plug with my problem employee was not only picturing the problems continuing, but also picturing the way that I wanted my business to be. I pictured what it would be like with someone in that position who was truly performing, how much better it would be. The more I pictured that, the more I saw it, the more I became determined to have what I wanted and the more I hated what I had. As Martin Luther King said, "I see a day . . ." That vision changed an entire nation and created a lot of endings to really bad realities. Whether in small matters or large ones, the method is the same.

So play the movie forward in both directions, negative and positive. Feel your vision, smell it, see it. See the reality that could be if you would only end what is. And see the reality of your future if you don't. That will get you moving. Also, *do this with your team.* Ask your team if they want to be where they are now a year from now or if they want a different reality. Then ask them what endings will be necessary to bring that about.

Create "Ending Alliances"

The reality of human behavior is that we are affected by those we are near. Recent research shows that even in patterns such as weight gain, whom you hang around with will affect you. If you have family or friends who are overweight, your chances of being overweight go up. If you live in a sober environment, you will have less chance of relapse. If you are creating a corporate culture that values urgency, you will move quickly to create endings that you need to create.

I see this in groups of leaders or in teams when I give them the assignment to figure out what endings each of them needs to create. When everyone believes in the urgency of needed endings, positive pressure to change gets created. The good, positive group pressure to get off the dime is strong, and it works. We need each other to create this kind of change. I just led an off-site session in which the guiding question I gave the clients was How will you create "heat" around this table? A team that "feels the heat" puts positive pressure on one another to perform.

If you are leading a change movement in a company, you must form power alliances, or what are often termed "powerful coalitions," people who will be the influencers of change. Whether their influence comes from a position of authority or from personal respect that they have earned, these people will keep the energy going to end what has been and create what is needed.

Recently I consulted with a CEO who wanted to drive change that had been lagging after many attempts; previous efforts had been delegated to one person, who had not gotten it done. We worked to get the power alliances together, the people who had influence throughout the organization, and created a structure in which they would have a lot of exposure, communication, and input to a lot of people. Their unity around the ending was contagious and became the group norm for the organization. For the first time, it became "not OK" to *not* be on board, whereas for the previous three years, being stalled had been fine.

It often helps to delegate part of the urgency mission and message to subteams of two or even to individuals, then make them accountable to the group for doing their part each week or at certain intervals. That way, they all have to regularly answer for their responsibilities. They own it as part of the team and get team pressure to get their part done. Who wants to go to that meeting unprepared?

In your own life, you need the same kind of power. Ask yourself this question: who am I surrounding myself with, day to day? Those who support and create energy for change? Or those who are stuck in the comfort of what is? Whether you want to re-create a company, or lose a hundred pounds, whom you surround yourself with is going to be a key factor. Do not ignore this truth, or you are very likely to stay stuck.

One of my favorite stories comes from a group of women I was working with. One of them was having particular difficulty breaking up with a boyfriend who was not good for her in the long term. She knew that but was unable to break it off. When she did attempt to end it, she would miss him, long for him, idealize the good times, and always go back, thereby putting off the life she dreamed of for the comfort of the current one that was frequently dissatisfying. Often, after a breakup, he would call her, and as they talked, she would remember his charming "good parts," as she put it. She would then long to be with him, he would invite her over, she would go, reconnect, stay the night, and hate herself the next day.

The group began to see this pattern over and over and started to exert good, positive pressure on her for an ending. They offered to be with her in the initial withdrawal stages. They confronted her with how she was settling for less than she wanted in a relationship. I could see the power of the alliance building. Then it happened.

She came to the group one day and told them that the night before, he had called her and begun another charm offensive, and she gave in. He invited her over and she said she would go, as she was certain that "they could make it work this time." He could be "so good," as she put it. But then she said, something else happened:

"As soon as I hung up the phone, I could hear all of you in my head! Your voices were so loud!" Pointing around the circle to different women, she said, "I could hear you saying, 'What are you thinking? He is just trying to use you again for sex! He won't deliver on the relationship!' And then you said, 'Don't give in to this again! He is not what you want!' And you, 'Why do you keep giving yourself to someone who is not the person you really want?'

"As your voices got louder, I picked up the phone, called him back, and said, 'I am not coming.' He tried to talk me into it, and I hung up as I said, 'Don't ever call me again.' It was your voices in my head that gave me the strength to do what I needed to do."

From brokenhearted girlfriends to addicts to CEOs, we need and are influenced and strengthened by the voices around us. So here is your question:

Who are your change agents, either for yourself or your company, for the endings that you need to make happen?

Create Vision

A few years ago, our family moved to a new home. My two daughters were five and seven at the time and loved the previous house. They had good friends in the old neighborhood, lots of great experiences, and loved their school; moving was the last thing they wanted to do. But it was a necessary ending that we needed to make, as we needed more space.

Consulting with the psychologist parent in me, I decided to begin the conversation with them when the idea first came up. "So, would you guys ever want to change houses? Maybe get one where you had your own playroom, or a flat yard where you could do a lot more fun stuff?" I asked, trying to sell a few of the benefits.

"No!" they said in unison. "Never! We love living here." I was truly taken aback at the passion that they came at me with. I was glad that they loved their home, but this did not bode well for our moving plans. I knew that it was not going to be an easy sell or an easy ending.

But then I had an idea. The new house was undergoing a total remodel and would be unlivable for many months. In that time period, there was enough room to do something sneaky. The new house, I knew, had a playhouse in the backyard, just perfect for them at their ages. So without telling them that they were moving, I just took them over there to "see a friend's house," and expose them to all the bennies, secretly.

When we went, I wandered around looking at all the construction and they immediately noticed the playhouse. They ran to it, went in it, and within minutes were taking snails into it, putting flowers in the window boxes, climbing on the roof, and doing a bunch of other things that showed real engagement. Then I told them we had to go, and they resisted, wanting to stay and play more. But I held firm, creating more desire for the forbidden fruit that I would one day want them to embrace.

Over the next few weeks, I continued to play this trick and even threw in a dip in the pool one time to seal the deal. Also, I took them upstairs to let them see the bedrooms and walk out on the balconies, and I employed other sneaky ways of getting them attached. I walked them to the park, which was right down the street, and talked about how close it was to that house. "Wow, wonder what it would be like to live that close to the park!" I said. "That must be really cool to just be able to walk to the park from your house! Those people are so lucky."

You get the picture. Gradually, keeping them close to the motivating vision, letting them experience it, taste it, feel it, and be in it, they were closer to embracing an ending than they knew. When they got the news, "We are moving," it was a shock, and they immediately protested. "No! We don't want to move."

But when they started to think about the playhouse, the pool, the park, their rooms, and so forth, the ending they were being asked to go through was not as impossible as it once would have been. They had "touched it," and it was tangible enough to get them through the change. This is similar to when heads of sales must get their salespeople to experience new products, touch them and feel them before they can shift to selling them with urgency.

Whenever people have to do a necessary ending, they need sustainable motivation. They have got to have enough fire in their bellies for the new to put an end to the old. Otherwise, when it gets tough, they want to go back and pull out of the change.

Remember Jack Welch's strategy for pruning? If a business could not be number one or number two in its market, it would be fixed, shut down, or sold. That is a vision to work toward. In creating any kind of change, continually holding up the picture of what you want it to be is essential to maintaining urgency. It creates cognitive dissonance with what is. It is the standard against which the current reality is judged, daily. So it keeps us moving toward the goal.

There is a good reason that direct-sales companies keep waving the sales prize before their salespeople. Or that the CEO overcommunicates the picture of what tomorrow is going to look like. Or that a woman keeps the Club Med bikini picture on the refrigerator, reminding her of the vacation that will be a lot more fun after she loses thirty pounds. Kind of makes opening that refrigerator door a little harder.

Although the very word *vision* and the techniques of seeing the "good future" have been so talked about that they almost fall on deaf ears at times, that overuse has happened for a good reason. Human brains are designed to create what they see in the future. Our internal resources begin to align with that internal reality and create it. It is the reason that great golfers see the shot before they hit it, or NBA players see the ball going in the basket before they shoot it. It is the reason that CEOs cast the vision of what they want the company to look like and be over and over. When people see it, they can create it. If it is communicated strongly enough and often enough, they almost cannot *not* create it!

But as it is overcommunicated, you also begin to realize that you can't have that vision if the current realities and practices continue to exist. You have to end them. Therefore, vision empowers necessary endings. I can't have B if I hang on to A. Somehow our conscious and unconscious forces work toward creating what we have envisioned. It has been proved over and over. The question Where do you picture yourself in five years? is more than an inquiry to find out more about a person. It may be diagnostic of where they will actually be.

So make it real. Write it down. Talk about it and create reminders in your personal life and your organization. Line your company's walls with pictures of the new reality. When you do that, the one they are living in every day won't be as welcome anymore.

Set Deadlines

This is rocket science that is not rocket science—rocket science because it works for very esoteric reasons, but not, because it should be obvious. Deadlines force endings when nothing else does. Ask a bankruptcy judge if they have any effect, or ask any CEO who has gone through a bankruptcy. Does your tax-return procrastination get weaker the closer it gets to April 15? You get the picture.

The rocket-science part involves the role of structure and the brain. We need structure to organize energy, contain it, and direct it toward an effect. It would be great if we all had the same level of self-discipline as some leaders, who create deadlines in their heads all the time. They live by them: "Today I have to get this or that done." High-performers live by a sense of urgency, which is necessary for any performance to happen. Even the writing of this book happened because I created monthly deadlines for myself for a certain amount of words or chapters to be done by that month. Otherwise, it would never, ever have happened.

But in the areas where we find that harder to do, like creating some difficult or painful endings, we need external deadlines. We need to "do the ending by January 1, period." Such a deadline forces urgency and gets us moving.

In other places, I have written about a friend who bought a company that he took from $25 million in revenues to over $500 million by an ending that he engineered as soon as he bought it. He ended 80 percent of the operations that the company was engaged in, because he thought the "real life" of the company was in about 20 percent of its operations. Although even the 80 percent was profitable, he saw the "best buds" in the 20 percent and pruned the rest. How?

He set a deadline for his management team and told them that he wanted that 80 percent gone by January 1. In June of the previous year, he told them they had six months to get out of those businesses. They protested: "We will lose money. We don't have enough time to get the best price." But he held firm. *Getting the best price for what you do not value is not the issue. Getting to what you do value is the issue. So, do it, no matter what, by a certain date. Time is the most important issue.* Sometimes there is bleeding when you cut out a cancer.

And they did it. The issue to keep before you is this: "They could have taken more time to *get a little more out of what they did not want.*" Think about that sentence. If you understand the absurdity of that statement, it will get you to create deadlines. If we always want more out of what we don't want or what is not working, we don't understand pruning at all.

Set a deadline for someone to hear what your expectations and demands are and for her to respond, and let her know that if the date passes without action, *you* will create an ending. Set a deadline for a person's performance to improve, and tell him that if it does not, he is gone. Set a deadline for a business unit to turn around, and let the people running know that if it doesn't by then, you'll shut it down. Set a deadline by which an initiative will get done, or the people in charge won't be in charge. Set a deadline for whatever it is that you need to change, and you focus energy and time together.

I recently heard a leader put it this way: "If I have someone who is not getting on board for a change we need to make, I meet with him or her first and try to understand their concerns. I hear them out and honestly try to take what they say to heart, and if it has merit, take the necessary steps, even if that means canning my plans. But, if it doesn't, and the team has worked on it as well, and that person is still dragging, I go back to them and have a conversation. I tell them that I understand that they have some real reservations, and I can respect that. *But I cannot have them putting their foot on the brake while I am putting mine on the accelerator.* So I tell them they have thirty days to figure out if they can get with it or not, and if not, I understand and wish them well. But they will have to leave if they can't get on board, because I can't have their foot on the brake on an ongoing basis."

Thirty days. Deadlines focus energy like a laser. They make movement happen, if they are real. Which brings up a point.

Remember, a deadline without consequences is not much of a deadline. So promise consequences for making and missing the deadline, and deliver them. If the deadline is for yourself, get someone involved who has the power to execute those consequences for you. It is the old, "Here is a check for a big amount. If I have not done *x* by this date, you are free to give it to someone I do not like." Ouch.

Question for you or your team: What endings do you need to set a deadline for?

Create Structure

Endings happen when we create the structure that drives them. Structure consists of time, plans, critical paths, milestones, deadlines, meetings, allocation and release of resources according to milestones, consequences for not meeting milestones, and other elements. The more years that I spend in leadership consulting, the more I value the role of creating structure that aligns with urgency around the vital, as well as getting rid of structure that keeps the nonvital going.

So when you want to end something and you have had difficulty doing it on your own, set up a structure. As in the process of change I talked about earlier, get an outside coach, accountability partner, peer, management team, or someone to sign up for a process, and put it into place: a structured process, not one in which "We'll do it when we get time." That won't happen.

Then add time structures to the process to help you execute your ending. Like the woman I talked about above who had a weekly group that she attended to help her through the breakup, get your regular meeting around change happening, so that you won't continue to "get to it when you can." You will never get to it that way, because you have internal and external forces working against getting to it at all. The external structure creates the rails for the train to run on.

For one executive I worked with, I created a meeting around a particular ending once a week, with specific milestones that his team had to meet each week. We aligned people, business initiatives, strategy, and other resources around this one agenda, and the structure of having a plan with a timetable got it done. But without this structure, as they would tell you, change had floundered for some time.

How bad do you want to change? Bad enough to create a structured plan to get it done? If so, your chances of ending whatever you need to end just went up. Ask any spouse who struggled for years with an addict who finally went to Al-Anon in a structured meeting, regularly, a few times a week, and they will tell you that that is what made the necessary ending happen.

This need for structure is satisfied in four tactics used by those who create urgency, listed by John Kotter in *A Sense of Urgency*. Such people, he writes, "behave with true urgency themselves *every single day*. They *do not* just say the right words daily, but more importantly, they make their deeds consistent with their words. They do so as visibly as possible, to as many people as possible, all in ways designed to reduce contentment with the status quo and the anxiety or anger that comes so easily with failures."

Kotter is correct in noting that this behavior must be consistent "every single day." Otherwise an ending won't happen, because the time-and-energy quotient we talked about earlier won't be strong enough. The question is how to do that "every day" thing. It is more likely to happen when it is in the schedule, with some structure and peer pressure and teeth to it, than when we are relying on the ones who are already resisting, even if they are we ourselves.

QUESTION: WHAT STRUCTURE—TIME, plans, and other factors—do you need to create in order to make sure your endings happen?

Stay Close to the Misery

Your brain doesn't move you toward pain, and yet the pain is one of your biggest and best motivators. If you are dentist phobic, even though you want healthy teeth, you avoid going as long as you can chomp on food without wincing. But when it starts to hurt at three A.M., you go the next day. Endings are like that. We tend to execute them when we get a tummy full of the misery. To the degree that we can stay distant from it, we don't get moving.

I once worked with a CEO in technology who had a significant need for an ending to an ongoing quality problem in his company. It was so significant that he had prioritized it as the number-one issue for their next five years' growth and competitive position. When I came on the scene, it had been a "focus" of his for about three years, yet no progress had been made. It had to do with some disconnects between the manufacturing side of the business and the service-delivery and customer-facing side, with the usual rock throwing that happens in those kinds of divides. Part of the problem was that the geographical homes of the departments were a thousand miles apart, and the two sides did not get together often enough.

The strategy had been for him to get together with the executives to whom he was delegating the issue, explaining to them how important it was and letting them work on it. In the interim, he would focus on the things that gave *him* energy, and this was not one of them. But they were not getting it done, and at various intervals, he would become aware all over again of its importance and get amped up about it. At that point, he would call them in and beat them up over it, but not much would happen until next time. It was classic "ignore and zap" leadership.

There was no sense of urgency for *them* to get it done, and he was not leading them through the time intervals, devoting the necessary time and energy. He was comfortably distant. Nor was he creating urgency around the need for the stall to be over with and progress to begin, other than his twice-a-year temper tantrums. But it was absolutely vital to the overall mission that this change happen. So we diagnosed his issue as exactly that: *he needed to create his own urgency around it and end the stall.* But how?

The main problem here was that he was too far away from the misery. He was
focused on the revenue side of the business and heavily involved in
acquisitions of new companies and marketing. So day to day, which
turned into month to month, he would have virtually no interface
with the one infected tooth that could bring the whole company
down. He was just "chewing on the other side of his mouth." So
I decided that we needed to make a rule to force him to chew on
the side that hurt, so he would finally go to the dentist and get this
tooth pulled.

I got him directly involved in experiencing the service problems
for himself. He sat in on customer help lines. He spent some time
visiting and talking to the service centers in the retail stores and
outlets, as well as time in workgroups hearing the kinds of problems that they were encountering with customers. Then he had to
hear the kinds of responses that the service people were getting
when they tried to take it to the product side and get the changes
done. It was maddening. When he did that and finally experienced
some of the walls that were in the way of getting changes made, he
got religion.

First he got mad, so I gave him a time-out, as anger doesn't
achieve much lasting change. But after he cooled off, he then began
to pull them all together, break down the walls between the two
divisions, and get them really understanding the issues from both
sides. Finally the sales team understood some of the issues that
the developers would run into when sales would request a "simple
fix." And the developers understood better that their fixes were
not working a lot of the time and that their answer on the phone of
"Well, it should work" did not make it so. And they finally got the
kinds of heartburn that those delays were causing the people who
actually had to deal with customers, and the pain that customers
themselves were experiencing. This stuff *really* mattered, but it had
been stalled for three years. *And one of the reasons was that the ones who*

could change it were too isolated from the pain of it all. When developers have to leave the science building and talk to a customer, it helps.

Then the breakthrough really happened. In getting close to the pain himself, the CEO found the beaver dam that was clogging up the river. It was an executive who was really standing in the way of change and had allowed a lot of these logjams to remain. After a short process of addressing it with him and getting little move-ment, the CEO made one of those Drucker "life and death" deci-sions for the business. He removed the executive from his position. And everything turned around. The necessary ending to the false hope that it was "going to get better" because he had told someone to go fix it finally died. He got to the good hopelessness we dis-cussed, and he executed a necessary ending to the problem. But it would have never happened if he had continued to *allow himself to remain detached from the problem.* I had to get him face-to-face with it, every day, until he got sick of it and what it was doing to his vision. Then he finally did something about it.

QUESTION: WHAT ISSUE are you shielding yourself from so that you are not close enough to the pain that you need to motivate you to change?

Measure, Measure, Measure

Closely related to staying close to the misery is the need for ongo-ing measurement. I continue to be surprised by how easy it is for any of us to ignore the passage of so much time between the times that we assess and measure the things that are most important to us. We think we did it yesterday, but it was months ago. I think it may have something to do with how fast-paced all of work and life is now, and the overwhelming amount of work that flies at us each day, with e-mail and the speed of information flow. We literally have too much to process and work on. With high-level leaders, this is an issue that I see increasingly as time moves on. They are overwhelmed. How is your inbox?

Whether that is a reason or just an excuse, often more time than we realize goes by since the last time we took the vital signs of what is most important to us. That creates a lack of urgency energy. When I was in the psychiatric treatment-center business, we would have to gear up in staffing and other resources for an increase in our adolescent services when the first school report cards were sent out to parents in the fall. For many parents, it was the first time in a long time that they got a picture of how their kids were really doing, and finally it created some urgency to put an end to the slide. They called for help. I am grateful for the daily and weekly reports that my daughters' school sends home for that reason. It keeps me "urgent" over their studies and other needs. Taking vital signs is a good thing.

It is likely that seasons are going by or branches need pruning and you don't know it, because of a lack of measurement. That is the nature of not being omniscient. But it is also the reason that we measure the things that are important to us, so that if there is disease or something that is not the best but is taking up resources, we can "fix, close, or sell." If we aren't measuring, we don't know.

Sam Walton was known for his measuring and monitoring systems, which kept a close watch on vital signs. If you use this kind of discipline, your brain will soon internalize this awareness, and you will feel more urgent around ongoing performance. Research shows that one of the important aspects of getting to the highest level of performance is the degree that someone gets immediate feedback. As a rule, the more immediate the feedback, the better the performance. Feedback helps create what well-known researcher Mihaly Csikszentmihalyi refers to as *flow*.

So measure and evaluate what you want to make grow. Be the inspecting gardener, and you will get healthy urgency to create quick endings before the problems get too big. Think teeth cleaning versus root canals. Planned deficits and slow growth are fine, and all the numbers don't always have to be happy. Sometimes bad numbers are in the plan. But in those instances, you are on an intentional plan, not headed for a train wreck. And you know the difference by diligent measuring.

Use Authority and Make an Executive Decision

I was talking to a seasoned CEO about this issue of creating urgency, and he agreed with me about the importance of all of the techniques we have been discussing. But he added an important one. He said, "Sometimes you just have to get authoritarian about it. That is why I like being in charge." He went on to explain what he meant: At times, teams find themselves in quandaries. They don't like the options available to them, so they just stay where they are and don't make a move. At those times, he said, you need to make an executive decision. I agreed.

He told me of a situation in his retail chain. In a downturn, sales were stuck at the bottom and were not moving. He checked in with management, and they told him all of the great things that they were doing—and they were. Marketing exploits, creativity, canvassing, motivational tricks, and so forth. They were doing it all but still no sales. So to this seasoned retailer, that could only mean one thing: *price.* To him, when something is not selling and still not selling, the price is too high. So he moved in.

He went to the division and told them that they were cutting prices. They rebelled. "No! We can't do that. We'll screw up all of our balance sheets, our financing relationships, our margins. . . ." They had a lot of reasons not to move on price, he said. But the bigger danger was that they would be sitting there six months from now with all of that inventory, really in trouble. So he said, "Cut it"—by a big margin. They did, and it began to move.

As he said, the turnaround never would have happened if he had not used his authority and made the executive decision that they did not want to hear about. At some point, if you are a leader, sometimes you have to lead, even when no one wants to follow. Alignment and other issues notwithstanding, there are those instances when you sometimes have to grab the wheel and exercise the authority that you have. Sometimes urgency is created when the sheriff rides into town.

Urgent Is the New Normal

Creating urgency around necessary endings is key to what happens with your time and energy. If those are your main resources, which they always are, then letting time go by without bringing urgent energy to change is going to ensure that your tomorrow will be the same as today. If stalled out is normal now, create urgency so that action is the new normal.

CHAPTER 9

Resistance: How to Tackle
Internal and External Barriers

I don't know what happens," Seth said. "I know there are issues that are vital to our mission, and I know I have to do them. I get really motivated to get them done, but somehow, I find myself procrastinating. I just kind of stall, even when I know it will be good to do. I don't know why I don't do what I know I need to do."

There are probably few leadership or performance consultants or coaches who have not had this kind of conversation. Getting un-stuck is a big felt need, and for good reason. We have already seen a lot of the reasons that stuckness exists, and in the previous chapter, we looked at how to get the energy focused to overcome this stuckness and move with greater urgency. But there is still one problem left in terms of getting on the right side of time: resistance. Sometimes you can get moving, have good energy, and then stall out all over again or at the very least, slow yourself down. In the interim, valuable time is being lost.

INCOMPATIBLE WISHES

In the last chapter, we saw how one CEO had to make an executive decision to overcome his management team's resistance to cutting prices. As he and I discussed this situation, the CEO said his team members were especially concerned about what lowering prices would do to their profit margins. They had hoped for and committed to a certain rate of return as a metric for success.

The problem was clear: *they had two incompatible wishes.* They wanted to increase revenues, which they were not getting because they had no sales at current pricing. And they wanted a certain rate of return. Both of those are great goals, but in the environment that they found themselves in, they couldn't have both. They could have sales, but they were going to have to forfeit the returns, because to get sales you would have to lower prices. That was reality.

The CEO saw this clearly, so it was easy for him to execute a decision. If you have no sales, you have no business. But members of his team were so married to their wish for certain financial performance that they could not get any sales going at all. So the wish for those numbers and the wish to have revenues now were incompatible. Therefore, they were stuck. Incompatible wishes are a formula for resistance.

Getting people to finally see the stark incompatibility of certain desires is often what finally gets them unstuck. Recently I met with a single woman who defined herself as stuck. She was in a relationship that was not all that she wanted, and she was chronically dissatisfied. He did not have the "drive" that she desired, which she saw as essential in order for her to "respect him." This guy was just not that type. So when I asked her why she didn't go after the kind that she wanted, she would say, "because I want *him*. I love *him*."

"But I thought you wanted someone who was more like the driver, achiever type," I said.

"I do, I know I do. But he is so great in other ways, and I love him. I want to be with him, too," she said.

"Too?" I asked.

She knew she was caught as soon as she said the word *too*. That is the issue: that sometimes we want two or more things that can't coexist. She wanted to be with an achiever and she wanted to be with him. But she could not have both of those wishes. Hanging on to both kept her from having either. Sometimes we can do this with a person, even an employee: "I want a high-performer, but I want to work with Joe," you might think. Well, make up your mind, because you can't have both. If you have a high-performer, it won't be Joe, and if you have Joe, you won't have a high-performer.

Here are some examples of incompatible wishes:

- I want to get the team moving, but I don't want to have to deal with the conflict that it is going to bring up.
- I want the margins that we need, but I also love the old product line that has the lower margins.
- I want a high-performer in this position, but I want Suzy's people skills.
- I want to meet with the team regularly, but I want to work from home.
- I want to have the highest performance in the company, but I also want time at home with my kids.
- I want more time with my buddies, but I also want to really work on my marriage.
- I want to achieve more toward some of my goals, but I want more time off.
- I want to invest my money, and I want that new car.
- I want to eat all the brownies, and I want to fit into my jeans.

Part of maturity is getting to the place where we can let go of one wish in order to have another. The immature mind "wants it all." But the truth is that the most valuable things come with a cost. To win, we have to give up some things for others.

So if you feel resistance about executing a certain ending, figure out what two or more desires are in conflict, admit to yourself that you can have only one, and then ask yourself this question:

Which one am I willing to give up to have the other one?

NO ATTACHMENT TO A CERTAIN OUTCOME

In my discussion with the CEO who forced the price cuts, I noticed a quality that I had seen in him before, and I highlighted it. "You know," I said, "you mention going in and making an executive decision as if that were the only key to making this work. But there is something else that was essential. Do you know what that was?"

"No, not offhand. What do you mean?" he asked.

"It is a quality I have noticed in you before, and I think it is central to your success. *It is your ability to not be attached to any particular outcome.* A person is able to cut prices or execute any other right move *only* if he is free and not attached to any specific outcome, like margins, for example. Otherwise, he is stuck," I said. "You are able to exercise the right choice because you are not overly attached to having it work out a particular way. Even though you want a particular result, you hold it loosely, do the right thing, and then don't let your worry stand in the way."

"Oh my," he said. "*That is probably the most important issue.* You can't get attached to any outcome. If you do, you won't ever be able to do what's best for the health and future of the business. Because doing the right thing sometimes can threaten all potential outcomes."

"Did you always have this quality from the time you started the company, or did you get more secure in it after you had less of a need to make any particular deal happen?" I asked, curious if it was the security of his significant wealth that afforded him that freedom or if the reverse was true. In other words, was it exactly that quality that had made his success and fortune, or can you be that free to do the right thing only if you can afford to? His answer confirmed my bias.

"I had it from childhood," he said. "It was a family value. You do the right thing, make the best choice, and 'let the chips fall where they may.' Otherwise, you will really get sideways. I have always been that way."

I was playing a movie in my head at that point of all of the great outcomes that derive from that stance. I could see thousands of negotiations in which he had been able to hold firm, refusing to give in to points that would not have been good for him or the business only because he *did not have to have the deal go through. He was not attached to the result. He could walk at any time if the conditions were not right.* That is power, the power to not do something destructive because you are so free from needing any outcome that you are not forced into wrong choices.

I could see bad deals that he had walked away from and people that he had stood firm with because he did not need a particular outcome, did not have to have any specific deal work, and as a result, he had avoided many bad positions and had secured many good ones. This is a fundamental truth about endings: *you have to be able to face losing some things you might want in order to be free to do the right thing. If you can't, you are stuck.*

In our discussion, he told me how true that principle had been for him, not only in business but personally, as well. He recalled a story of a crossroads in a personal relationship many years ago where he had taken a similar stand, not knowing what the outcome would be, and how it solidified the relationship, which continued for many years. He had a business partner with whom he had to draw a hard line: "Change our deal to exclusive, or I can no longer be your partner." He could not have taken that stand if he were not free from the outcome, i.e., he had to be willing to let the partner walk. Likewise, if the spouse of an addict is too attached to having her stay, he can't do the right thing and say, "Get off drugs or get out." You have to be able to let go of the very thing, sometimes the very person, that the right choice may cause you to lose. "I need you to commit or go away."

Here's another way to say it: you can't do the prudent thing if you cannot stand for it all to fall apart. Often, in necessary endings, you have to give something up or be willing to lose something in order to gain it. If there is a destructive pattern in a relationship, for example, and you want to take a stand to end it but refuse to do so out of the fear that the other person may walk away, then you are stuck. As the CEO put it, you have to be able to "let the chips fall where they may."

Sometimes people leave, customers go away, others are upset, or alliances are broken. And often those are huge losses. But staying stuck can be even more destructive in the long run. Detachment from any one outcome is a common trait that all great performers have in common. Here is your question:

What particular outcome are you unwilling to sacrifice to realize your vision of the future?

MEDICATING THOUGHTS

Have you ever had a friend who was a hoarder? You're probably familiar with the resistance that happens when you try to get that person to throw away something that is serving no purpose but taking up space in the garage. What is it that keeps people from throwing things away that they need to get rid of? Usually, it's one of two thoughts: *I might need that* or *I will miss it.*

Consider a scenario in which one friend is helping another clean out an attic or garage. You might hear a dialogue that goes something like this.

"Here, let's get rid of the stuff in this box. You don't use this anymore."

"No, I want to keep that," the hoarder says. "Don't throw that box away."

"How long has it been since you used these things?" asks the friend.

"I don't know, probably about twenty years."

"So why don't you get rid of them?"

"Because I might need them."

In the same scenario, you might also hear an exchange like this.

"I'm throwing this away," the friend says. "It's just trash."

"Don't throw that away!" screams the hoarder. "That's Johnny's first poopy diaper! I will miss it! It reminds me of how cute he was as a baby."

The thought that keeps your friend a hoarder is something akin to *I love that item, and I will miss it too much if it is gone.* (By the way, that's what memories are for . . . so you don't have to keep everything.)

These two thoughts, *I might need that* and *I will miss it* are examples of "medicating thoughts." For hoarders, medicating thoughts numb the anxiety that comes from making a decision to part with something they are attached to. They experience anxiety when they hit the moment of truth and know that it is time for an ending, but they get rid of the anxiety by giving themselves a good reason not to act. They think, "I may need that. It makes total sense to keep it." Or "Because I will miss it too much, it has to stay. No one would throw anything away that means as much to them as that diaper means to me." Back in the box it goes, and the anxiety is gone until next time. When did "missing" become a criterion for what has value?

---

*The hoarder mentality thrives not only in garages,
but in business and people's lives, as well.*

I was talking to an executive recently who had to fight with his management team to close down a division of the company that he said was only breaking even. His team had always managed to find enough revenue to make the division pay for itself, he said, but it was clear that the unit was "really not a business that was going anywhere. And it was certainly not core to what we do. But it was taking focus away for some key people, and we needed them to focus on what was truly core and had a future."

"Why didn't they want to give it up?" I asked.

"Because they kept saying to themselves, *But it might make money, and since we aren't losing money on it, let's keep it to see if it turns around,*" he said.

"Classic hoarding behavior in the business sense," I said. "Hoarders always say, 'I might need that' in one form or another. This is the business example of hoarding. 'We might need that business next year if it gets good.' It is like saying, 'If we had some ham, we could make some ham and eggs, if we had some eggs.' The only thing holding it together is a *might* or an *if*, with no reason to support it."

"Exactly," he said. "Get rid of it and get focused on what is real, I told them. No room for *it might.*"

He had created billions in revenues, and I've seen his clean garage. The same quality probably created both.

The idea here is that when it is time to execute an ending, people resist by telling themselves a whole host of soothing sentiments that calm them down and do away with the urgency. The urgency they feel from seeing reality gets them close to pulling the trigger, and that makes them anxious. So to rid themselves of the anxiety, they talk themselves out of action. "I might need that, or him, or it."

Likewise, getting to a point of follow-through requires that you observe yourself when you make such statements and become aware of the ways that you are lying to yourself. Here are some common ones:

"I'll Do It Later"

Later is one of the most abused drugs we have available to us. Very few medicating thoughts can rid us of the anxiety associated with a difficult action better than to tell ourselves that we will do it "later." It kind of makes it all go away. Why? Because when we say it, we think we are actually *going* to do it "later," so we feel the momentary relief of the problem being solved without having to go through the work to do the ending. The person bingeing on the buffet at holiday parties comforts himself with the thought that *after New Year's, I am going to go on a diet. See, there is really no problem eating all of this stuff now, because I am going to lose it, come January.* "Later" is as good as done, in his mind. But "January" never comes.

Leaders often do the same thing when they come face-to-face with a difficult business decision. They convince themselves of the need to follow through with that decision, know that it is necessary, and tell themselves that they will do it "after we get done with the new release. That is the first priority now." So they feel good about taking action *in their heads* as they plan to do it and feel relieved. But the reality is that it is not done, and the next time it comes up on the radar, they will engage in the same trick of resistance, and the ending will not occur. It is only a trick.

People in difficult relationships find many ways to play the "later" card. When they know that something has to change, they calm their internal dissonance with the thought that they *certainly* are going to address it, "just not today. I will do it when the timing is right."

When you come face-to-face with reality and realize you need to execute an ending, take note of whenever you tell yourself some version of "later." Here are some questions to ask yourself:

- If you are going to do it "later," then when will that be? Set a date.
- What real reason do you have for waiting? What specific information are you waiting on that is absolutely necessary to have before you make a move? Or what event must happen first before you can make the move? If there is not a real contingency, then why are you waiting?

If you are going to wait, set the deadline and bring someone into that decision to hold you accountable to it on that date. If possible, establish some consequences. Create a calendar about the costs of waiting. Make yourself look directly into exactly what that extra time is going to cost you, in money, energy, missed opportunities, or more misery. Then sign a contract with yourself every day that says "in exchange for not having to do this today, I will pay the following amount." Then list all of those costs. You are going to pay them anyway if you wait, so you might as well have it in writing. This is also a great team exercise. When people are throwing up resistances to a certain decision, have everyone sign off on the consequences as a group.

Selective Memory

"So why don't you tell him that you want to break up with him?" I asked Monica about her boyfriend, Stan. "You keep telling me over and over about this issue that just doesn't go away."

"Because he has so many wonderful qualities," she said. "There are so many things I love about him."

"Like what?" I asked.

"Well, like his sense of humor, and his charm. I still get excited whenever he is around. I am so drawn to him," she said.

"Yeah, I know." I empathized. "And then when you get together, what happens?"

"We have a great time," she said. "That is why it is so hard."

"You have a great time for how long?" I pushed.

"Well, when he is there. And then when we get together again," she said.

"And . . . when is that?" I asked.

"Too long . . ." she said, reflecting the truth that Stan would dip into her life with fly-by romance and investment and then be totally unavailable in any kind of sustained way that would build a true relationship.

"And then what happens?" I asked further, knowing the answer.

"I've told you. I call him and tell him how I am feeling ignored, and he gets mad and defensive and says that I am smothering him," she said.

"And," I reminded her, "he has the same reaction any other time you want to discuss an issue also. He gets defensive if you call him on anything."

"Yeah, I know," she nodded.

"So the reality is that all of these wonderful qualities that you will miss *are just one part of him.* They coexist with a lot of other qualities that make it impossible to have a relationship with him. You realize that, over and over, get depressed about it, and then know that you cannot continue that way. So you decide to end it. And then, you play a trick," I explained.

"What trick?" she asked.

"It is called the 'I will only think of the good parts of him' trick, so you won't have to do the breakup. Every time you think about breaking up, you begin to miss someone that does not exist, the Stan with only those good parts. If that were who he really was, you wouldn't be so dissatisfied.

"But the one you are missing, the one with only the wonderful qualities, *doesn't exist in real life*. The real Stan, the one with all of those good qualities, is the same one who continually frustrates you with his lack of commitment and other problems and qualities. He has other qualities besides the ones you like. That is the whole person, the whole picture that you must agree to like or not. But you keep focusing on only the good parts," I said. "You have selective memory when you think of breaking up with him. Then you miss someone who doesn't exist, and you think, *I can't break up with him. He is so wonderful*. But, the wonder is not the whole picture."

This is a well-known psychological defense that happens when people can't let go of a person or thing they are invested in. They idealize the lost or soon-to-be lost love object, instead of seeing it as a whole. They focus just on the part that they like and fail to take into account the negatives that make the good parts unusable. So they are never able to let go, because they feel that all they are letting go of is something wonderful. "He is so wonderful," should really be stated as, "He is so wonderful, but he is also unfaithful and a crook. I can't live with all of that."

Businesses do this sometimes with employees and with business units. They just look at the potential or the great aspects that they love and are excited about, and they find a way to negate the reality of all the downsides, especially the costs. The closer they get to making the decision, the more they focus on the good side of the ledger, and forget the whole picture. And resistance emerges as they go through lots of internal negotiations, trying to find a way to make it work so they don't lose all of what they love. They are bargaining with themselves to avoid the loss.

The truth may be that you have already negotiated those realities a thousand times and if you could have fixed it by now, it would be fixed. To get over the resistance, you have to continually keep the whole picture right in front of your eyes. Stay focused on the entirety. "Yes, he is talented, and to have his talent, we have to also have an awful culture. Do we want *both of those?*"

Questions:

- As you get closer to the decision, do you find yourself focusing on the positives and already anticipate missing those aspects?
- Do you forget or lose sight of all of the negatives?
- Do you minimize the negatives?

If this mechanism is where your resistance is coming from, get back into a mind-set of seeing the *whole* picture. Focus on all of the person or the business or the situation. Keep the negatives front and center; do not let them disappear, and you will retain your urgency and move more quickly.

THE PARADOX OF "WHOLE VISION"

My emphasis on seeing the whole picture may sound as though I'm saying you should have no tolerance for a relationship, employee, business, or anything that makes the picture less than perfect. In other words, "If he/she/it has negative qualities, we need to execute an ending and find a better he/she/it."

In fact, I am saying the opposite. The longest-lasting and best relationships, as well as the best businesses, are the ones in which everyone involved sees and loves the whole picture, positive and negative. In marriage, for example, you must love the whole person just as they are, warts and all, and maintain positive attachment. But that only happens with people who have the capacity to see the whole picture at once and still keep the love alive. It does not mean that we do not work on the warts, but it does mean that they are OK in the bigger scheme of things.

Seeing the whole picture is also the same quality that allows people to let go of the ones that should be let go of. The maturity to discern when to remain invested in a relationship or situation and when to let go of one is the same. You have to be able to see the whole reality in both situations, the one that you keep and the one that you don't. Otherwise, lasting relationships cannot happen, and bad ones cannot end. If we look at it all and love it, that is great. It means we are willing to deal with the negatives to have the positives. That is commitment. Conversely, if we look at it all and don't love it, there is an ending needed, because something about the negatives is a deal breaker. Same ability, different outcomes.

Businesses, for example, only thrive when leadership can see the good aspects, the potential, and at the same time embrace the obstacles and the problems that have to be solved to bring those potentials to fruition. That is mature leadership, the ability to see and work with the whole picture.

It is only when a person can see the whole picture and work with it as it is that lasting success happens. For example, take the Hollywood romance: The tabloids recount how a particular pair of celebrities discovered they are "soul mates" on the movie set, and the story is all about how wonderful their love is and how it will last forever. Six months later, the same tabloid chronicles the breakup of their perfect relationship. Why? Often because there is a romantic idealization happening in the beginning of the relationships. Each falls in love with an idealized fantasy of each other; each sees only the good and none of the bad. Then, when less-than-perfect qualities come into view, what happens? They lose touch with the good things they fell in love with and cannot handle the letdown. Instead of metabolizing the fact that their relationship has some faults, instead of working through those issues, they create an unnecessary ending.

Many personal and business failures come from just this dynamic: each party overidealizes the other, blocking out the negative, then later sees only the negative and blocks out the positive; one or both parties becoming motivated to toss it all. This is not maturity. Maturity is always about seeing both, the positive and the negative, and dealing with all of it. Sometimes that sum total is "good enough," but sometimes it is not, and an ending must occur. But you really won't know which situation applies—and you will suffer from both false positives and false negatives—unless you can see the whole picture in reality.

EXTERNAL RESISTANCES

Most of what we have discussed so far concerns internal resistances, the ones that occur within our own heads. But remember, just because you aren't paranoid doesn't mean they aren't out to get you. Most times when you exercise an ending of some sort, there will be people in your circle who will try to fight it or slow it down. You have to be ready for that to occur, recognize it as inevitable, and deal with it. Otherwise, other people will be in control of your life and decisions.

External resistances are those that come from other people. Their challenges and questions are not the helpful kind that a good confidante might provide. Sometimes the people in our business and personal lives who care about us actually stop or hinder us from making decisions they believe are not good for us. Right or wrong, they are acting out of what they believe are our best interests. That is not the kind of resistance I am referring to here. I am referring to resistance from people who have ulterior, self-protective, or self-interested motives. Let's look at some of these resisters.

Self-absorbed Resisters

Sometimes people put up resistance because your decision is going to affect them in some way and they do not want that change. It is like the situation where the CEO comes in and says, "We have an incredible opportunity to acquire XYZ Co.! It is going to triple our size and speed up our path to realizing our vision! This is the day we have been waiting for." Then, someone raises her hand and asks, "If we move, does it mean that I will lose my window?"

As ridiculous as that example is, it illustrates something that happens every day. Many times there are endings that are going to affect someone, and that person does not have the kind of character to put his self-interest aside and see what is good for the company or the mission. Passively or actively, this person is on a sabotage mission and is not looking out for you.

This type of person can appear friendly, offering "advice" to "help" you, but he is really a wolf in sheep's clothing. He will warn you of all of the downsides, all that can go wrong, what you will lose, and so on. Certainly there are times when we need that kind of advice, but this is not one of them. The situation I am referring to is one where this is not advice, but an attempt to keep you from going forward.

Threatened Resisters

Other times, the resistance comes from someone who is threatened personally by what you are doing. For example, when an addict begins to get sober, addict friends will try to get him to come back and party again because they see the person making the kind of change that they know they need but are afraid to make. So they try to do away with the threat to change that is standing right in front of them by luring him back to being like them.

Whether in business or personal life, when you do something difficult but worthy, it confronts people with their own lives. It activates all of their fears, and they quickly try to tell you the same things that they tell themselves. "It will never work. I know a lot of people who tried to do that, and they were sorry in the end." The truth is that they are stuck, you are getting unstuck, and you cause them to look in the mirror and face themselves. Unconsciously, they realize, *If she can do it, I could do it too. But to think about doing that scares me. I think I will talk her out of it, and then we will both be comfortable again.*

So watch for these resisters. Listen to them, weigh their reasons, ask them why they feel that way. Ask them also how they feel about the reality of what happens if you *don't* make the necessary change, and see what they say when you "play the movie" for them and ask them, "Do you really want that to happen to me?" See if they can look you in the eye and wish that upon you. Thank them for their opinions, then tell them, "I understand why you feel that way. But I have come to a different conclusion. I need to do this for me [or us, or the company]."

The NoNos

I love John Kotter's classification of the kind of person he calls the NoNo. He contrasts them with skeptics. Skeptics oppose change because they have real questions and problems with the change, but they are open to being convinced. NoNos, he says, are "highly skilled urgency killers. If they cannot undermine attempts at diminishing a contentment with the status quo, they create anxiety or anger and the flurry of useless activity associated with a false sense of urgency" [John Kotter, *A Sense of Urgency*]. In other words, they are entrenched against change and are not open to having their minds changed under any circumstances.

There are many motivators for NoNos. As a psychologist, I can tell you that I have seen them in many instances, and in my opinion, they can be pretty inflexible. They often are not open to what we call "assimilation and accommodation," a process by which normal people take in new data, accommodate ourselves to it, and change our minds. Not so with NoNos. Instead of taking in new data, they have all sorts of reasons for rejecting it, devaluing it, and undermining any accommodation that anyone would be close to making with it. So I agree with Kotter's good advice: *don't engage them.*

When you engage a NoNo or anyone else who is not listening (see the previous chapter on dealing with fools), you are de facto losing. They are trying to stall you, and they are not going to change, so to spend any time trying to convince them is to allow them to use their strategy of derailing. If you are talking to them, they are winning.

What Kotter suggests is to not ignore them but deal with them. His three strategies are to distract them, push them out of the organization, or expose them to the power of the group. In my experience, those are good suggestions, but in addition, the big idea I want you to get from them is that working with NoNos is not going to help. They are not interested in changing, in information, or in anything related to reality. You have to deal with them if they are in the way.

If you are in an organization or even an extended family or social circle, NoNos will by definition be against the change that you are trying to make. Understand that, and deal with it as the obstacle it truly is.

Stuff Happens When You Change

For every action, there is an equal and opposite reaction. When you make a move down a new path, obstacles will come as a result. Getting things done is hard, or more people would be doing it. So accept the fact that endings are difficult and hard to implement.

You will be going through new waters, and there will be waves. Big bumpy ones. It takes courage and perseverance to keep going.

In an upcoming section, we will examine some ingredients that will help you sustain the change. But for now, just know that when you hit obstacles, they might just be a good sign that you have done the right thing. It means that you are really making an ending and are merely encountering the tasks of the new season. But now that you have normalized a worldview of seasons, you are ready for that, and it won't surprise you.

CHAPTER 10

No More Mr. Bad Guy: The Magic of Self-Selection

My friend was struggling over what to do with her boyfriend of over a year. She was very attached to him, and "loved him deeply," as she said over and over in our conversations. "Then why the struggle?" I asked.

"He is not the kind of man I want to start a family with. I love him and love to be with him. He has the purest heart I have ever seen, and I love that about him. He is the smartest person I have ever known, and I love that about him. But he has no drive in life. He just gets by on his smarts and has no real initiative or plans for the future. He is a lot like a college student, not thinking much past the weekend," she said. "I need someone who will take charge and who will be a strong husband and father. I don't need a little boy that I 'mother' all the time."

"Give me some examples."

"Well, he is so talented that he gets freelance work and makes enough to live working about half-time. So the rest of the time, he sleeps in, plays computer games, and isn't productive. He is so smart that he can get away with it, but I want to see someone who attacks life and has some drive," she said.

"Plus, he lets me be too in charge. He doesn't make plans or take care of things like a real adult would. I don't want to be the one worrying about the future all the time. I want someone to partner with me so I feel secure."

"So what are you going to do?" I asked.

"That's where I'm stuck. I don't know what to do. I love him and do not want to break up with him, but I can't see myself marrying him until he changes. We talk about it, and then there is a little movement, but if I am not always nagging him, it does not change for long. Plus, I don't like it that he still gets high at his age. He should have outgrown that."

"Sounds like you feel like you have a tough decision to make. Why don't you let him make the decision?" I asked.

"What do you mean?"

"Well, you are kind of stuck because you think you have to decide on whether or not he is the right one or not. I don't think that is your decision to make. *I think it is his.*"

"What do you mean?" she asked.

"Your decision is to decide what kind of person you want to be married to. And it sounds like you know. Someone who takes initiative, is responsible, will step up and take charge of planning and worry about the future. Someone who values goals and uses his time well to build the kind of life you want together. Someone who is not using drugs. Basic adult kind of stuff.

"And his decision is whether or not he wants to be that person. That is a decision that only he can make, not you. So tell him that. Tell him what you want, and then tell him he gets to decide if he wants to be that person and be with you or not. That is up to him, as he is the only one who can control that outcome," I said.

"Keep going," she said. "I think I am getting it."

"OK," I said. "Just say something like this: Taylor, I have been thinking about my future and what I want long-term, the kind of man I want to be with for life and to start a family with. Here is what he will look like: He will be loving, smart, fun, and someone I connect well with, and he'll have my same values. Also, he will be responsible, will think about the future, will be going somewhere, and will be a good provider. He will take care of the basic things, like being financially responsible, and normal things that adults do. That is what I am looking for and that is the kind of person I will be with.

"Right now, that is not you. I love you, and I want that person to be you, but right now, it is not. So I can't see a future together as things are now. But I am going to give you a choice: you get to decide whether or not you want to be that person. If you do, and you become that kind of person and prove it to me long enough that I really can believe it, I would love to be with you. But it is up to you whether or not that is who you want to be and whether or not you want to be with me. It is your decision."

I could see in her expression that her mood had lifted. As we talked, she said that part of it was the clarity of just saying what she wanted. But another part was the relief of not being the "bad guy" by rejecting someone she loved or feeling that she was judging him. She did not want to judge him, as he was truly a good guy, and she loved and respected so much about him. She was tired of being in the position of feeling like the nagging judge. This approach re-lieved her of that responsibility, as it put him in charge.

He would be the one to decide whether or not he wanted to be with her. She set the standards for what being with her meant, and he could decide whether or not it was a match. It was his deci-sion, and he could self-select. Good for her as she did not have to judge anymore. Instead, her standards would be the judge. Good for him, as she was no longer going to nag but instead would let him decide whether or not he wanted to be with her in the ways that she required. No bad guy anywhere. Everyone was free again.

SELF-SELECTION

I find that in getting to a necessary ending, many people stall out for the same reason my friend was stuck. They do not want to be in the position of being the bad guy, rejecting someone or saying that person is not "good enough" in some way. It makes them feel bad and is a horrible dynamic in a relationship. Self-selection is the better way.

What it does is set a standard for what you want, regardless of what particular individual you are dealing with. Then the person gets to choose whether or not she wants to meet that standard. She self-selects. It's not much different from what happens in college admissions: Administrators at a good college are not being mean or judgmental when they set a minimum grade level for admission, but the requirement does make their standards clear. It defines the institution, leaving students to ask themselves if they want to go to that college, knowing that it means meeting that standard. They self-select.

Similarly, if you have an employee who is not performing, you might feel the same sense of being stuck that my friend did. You like the person and don't want to be the bad guy, firing him. So let him self-select.

"Terry, I want to talk to you about this position. The kind of person that I want to be in that chair is going to look like this: puts time and energy into building a team, is ahead of the curve in future quarters' planning and business generation, achieves a yearly growth rate in sales of x percent. Right now, you are not that person. I want you to be that person, and I hope you choose to become that person. But that is up to you. I want you to think about it and let me know if you want to do that and what your plan is to show me that you have become that person. I hope you do."

This is a totally different kind of ending. It has two outcomes—

one guaranteed, the other unknown and hopeful. The guaranteed ending is that you have put an end to whatever it was that you needed to prune from your life or business. In my friend's example, she put an end to being with someone who was not going to fit the bill as the kind of husband she wanted. In the employee example, it put an end to the performance problem. So the ending is created by the standard. That is guaranteed.

What makes the ending unknown and hopeful is whether or not the particular person is going to step up to the standards set. When we establish a standard, we have drawn a line in the sand for people to deal with. Whether or not they will is up to them. It is unknown and hopeful because sometimes they do. Other times, they don't. Either way, the pruning has happened, and you did not reject anyone.

SELF-SELECTION FOR YOUR OWN ATTACHMENTS

Another person you sometimes have difficulty saying no to might be yourself. In business and life, we have to be our own bad guy at times and say, "No, you can't have that" or "Do that." But we get attached to certain strategies, hopes, projects, businesses, or whatever. And we go back and forth, using all of the resistance strategy that I introduced in the earlier chapters. "Should I or should I not shut this down? Should I give it more time? It might . . ." And we stay stuck.

Self-selection for yourself works the same way. Set the standard: "If the business has not turned a profit by the end of this year, I shut it down." Or "If I have not found the job I want by June 1, I will call it quits and move." I live in L.A. and know many people who are trying to make it in the entertainment or music industry. Some of them have been trying for a while. When to quit? In my opinion, the smart ones have a date out there somewhere. "If I am not making a living at this by _____, I will give it up and go back to grad school."

Some people have a problem with such an approach, saying they might be selling themselves short. But I did not say the time period had to be short. I just said that it is a good idea to know how much of your life or resources you want to spend on something before you lose them all. What matters is that you are in charge, and sometimes having a standard to self-select against takes the decision out of your head and makes it objective, similar to Jack Welch's "Be number one or two in the market, or fix it, sell it, or shut it down."

CHAPTER 11

Having the Conversation:
Strategies for Ending Things Well

"H ave you talked to him yet?" I asked Lori, a leader in an advertising firm.

I was referring to Jeff, her direct report who had been heading a substantial division of their business and was responsible for working with various media platforms. Lori had just been recruited to another company, much larger and with much greater opportunity. She was going to be able to build her new team at the new company, and everyone assumed that Jeff would follow her wherever she went. Jeff had been her number-one person for seven years. They were pretty tight for a number of reasons.

First, Jeff was extremely competent in the math of it all. He could build models that used complicated formulas to find the best media buys and coordinate releases in a way that maximized returns for their clients. That meant lots of continued business and better bottom-line returns.

Second, Jeff was a bit of an eccentric character and did not let many people into his confidence. He kept them at a distance with an exterior that came off as arrogant and condescending. But Lori had an extreme gift in emotional intelligence (I told her many times she should have been a shrink if she had not been such a good executive) and because of that had won Jeff's trust over the years. She was one of the few people he had let into his life. As a result, she had gotten a lot of benefits over the last several years, not only from their friendship, but also from his incredible brain. What they had accomplished was superior. And there was a great deal of loyalty shared between the two of them.

But she had paid a price for that accomplishment. Jeff had two worlds inside the organization: those he treated well and those he treated despicably. He was one of those people that psychologists would describe as using a lot of *splitting* as a defense against his insecurity. He would divide the world into good guys and bad guys and treat them accordingly. If you had ever offended him or gotten on his bad side for any reason, forget it. There was little chance that you could get back in.

Over the years, Jeff's behavior had created a culture that was often fractured, making some projects difficult to navigate, and many people thought he was a real jerk. More often than she would like to admit, Lori found herself in the position of smoothing over situations with the people Jeff had offended. Too often she felt more like a therapist than an executive, and as good as Jeff was, she came to resent it. In addition, sometimes even with her, his "paranoia," as she called it would get aroused if his feelings were hurt or he felt slighted, and she would have to spend time and energy wooing him back.

After a lot of coaching conversations and soul searching, Lori reached a conclusion. Though Jeff was talented and smart, she was not going to take him with her to the new company. When she really got honest with herself, she admitted she was tired of having to deal with all of the collateral damage that Jeff caused, and all of the time and energy that she spent dancing around his issues.

She had a vision of having a new deputy who was easier to work with, or at least someone who created less drama. Once she saw this vision of the future, she felt "like a weight has been lifted," she said. Until . . .

"No, I haven't told him," she replied. "No . . ." The last *no* came with a heavy sigh and a look into the distance.

"Why?" I asked her.

"I don't know. I mean, I do know. It is going to be a nightmare telling him. He is not going to take this well at all. And I understand. After all, he has been my right arm for a long time. But he really has little clue how hard it has been for me, so he is just going to interpret this as me screwing him over, and it will reinforce his view that the world is not trustworthy," she went on. "I am dreading it."

As a coach, I have had that same conversation with scores of other people, as they stalled out in either a personal or professional context. Why did the ending stall? After all the deciding had been done, and they were *certain* that they needed to go forward, they still sat on it. Not because they were unsure or were afraid of the future. Not because they second-guessed their decisions or their mental maps prevented them from making it. The reason?

They dreaded the conversation.

They tell me it is the conversation itself, as well as the potential aftermath with the person in some instances, that stops them cold. They say that they play it over and over in their heads, and see it going badly, imagining all the worst scenarios. Add that to some of the mental maps we discussed before—endings are personal failures; endings make you mean; endings hurt other people—and you can see the appeal of not going through with a necessary ending.

What gets them through it? One key ingredient is *to be prepared for the conversation itself.* That preparation can make all the difference in the world. It can provide the confidence and the skills needed to finally pull the trigger. Let's look at how you can be prepared for the difficult conversation of a necessary ending.

BEGIN WITH THE END IN MIND

With the more difficult endings, there are usually a few issues that sidetrack the conversation. People may get off-mission in the midst of the endings conversation. They go into it thinking that they will tell someone that "it's over," whatever "it" is, but once they get in there, one of two things happens. They may get sidetracked by their attachment to the person or whatever else is the issue; then they "refeel" all of their love for the person or the project. They feel how fond they are of the person or the good sides of the business, and somehow they get engaged in talking about those, which invariably leads to the familiar wish: "Can't we find a way to make this work somehow?"

Then the conversation goes down the path of finding a way to "work it out." Never mind that the person doing the ending has spent months or more getting sure about the ending, having obsessed over all the back-and-forth a million times. But something about getting to that moment of actually making it happen makes people squishy once again. I remember one time when a board sent a CEO to fire someone and he came back having extended the person's contract! I said to him, "You went to break up, and you came back engaged! Not good!" But it happens.

The other thing that often happens in the ending conversation is that the ender runs into resistance from the endee and loses the verbal joust. Being more adept at the conversational dance, the endee talks the ender out of the ending.

Neither of these derailments is good, but both can be prevented with a little advance work and training. The work consists first of "beginning with the end in mind." Before you have the conversation, make sure you are clear in your head what you want the result of the conversation to be. Have specific goals for the conversation. Here are some examples:

- I want to leave the conversation with zero confusion, complete confidence that this is over.
- I want to leave the conversation having said that I care about the person.
- I want to leave the conversation letting the person know that although this is over, I want to keep in touch in case another opportunity opens up.
- I want to leave the conversation with the person knowing that although the project is over, I want the relationship to continue.
- I want to leave the conversation having said very clearly not only that it is over, but also why.
- I want to leave the conversation having said that I want absolutely no further relationship or contact with the person.
- I want to leave the conversation having said that if the person ever contacts me again, I will call the police.
- I want to leave the conversation having said that I do not want the relationship to end at all. What I want to end is a pattern, but it is her choice whether or not she wants to continue, and if she does, she will have to fulfill certain requirements.

While there are other possibilities, you get the gist. These are difficult conversations to have, and if you are not clear in your own head what you want to make absolutely sure you have said when it is over, chances are you won't say it. The results of that could be that you have no ending at all, only more ongoing confusion. Make a pact with yourself, "I promise I will not end the conversation until I have clarity on what I went there to say and do."

INTEGRATE CARE AND TRUTH INSIDE YOURSELF

If the reason that you are hesitant about the conversation is that you are afraid of hurting someone, as is often the case, the best preparation you can have is to "get integrated" inside yourself before the conversation. Your sense of concern for the person must be integrated with the truth of what you need to say.

Usually, when someone cares about how a person feels, there is the temptation to go squishy on the truth, because the truth hurts. So we tend to get a bit codependent in these kinds of conversations, not saying all that needs to be said for fear of hurting the person. The truth suffers, and often the ending gets flimsy.

On the other hand, if you are insensitive to people and just interested in the "truth" and dealing with reality, you might really hurt someone needlessly. Even if you don't care, it is still to your advantage to get this right and begin to care, because if you don't, it has a much greater chance of going bad.

So before you begin the conversation, get in touch with both sides, your concern for the other person and for the truth. Remind yourself that you care about the person and truly want the best for him. Feel your caring and empathize with how hard the truth may be for him to hear. As you do that, understand that the truth is always our guide. If something is not right for one party, it is not right for the other one, either. If it is not best for a team to keep someone on, it is really not the best place for that person, either. It is a mismatch. The truth is painful but best in the end.

If the reason for the ending is that the person is not performing well, you do a person no favor by giving her a position she does not deserve or not being honest with her about her shortcomings. You are robbing her of the chance to get better. So if you care, you will want to have the conversation truthfully as an expression not only of the truth, but also of that very caring. Think Simon Cowell plus some TLC.

Just as in pulling a tooth, quickly and thoroughly is usually best. Commit yourself to being honest and clear, and don't drag it out through a labyrinth of explanations, excuses, and less-than-honest patronization. Plan to just be nice and tell it the way it is, with a lot of compassion. Kind but true.

If you can get clear inside about your caring and the need for the truth, then you will do a much better job, which will allow you to go forward with less resistance. Feeling your concern will actually make you less afraid to speak truthfully, as you will know that you are not doing anything mean. And your truth will help you to be clear and helpful in what you say, and satisfy the need inside of you and the situation itself. It is like sharpening a knife to do the best surgery possible.

PRACTICE AND ROLE-PLAY IF NECESSARY

It may seem cheesy, but practice can be very helpful. Ask someone you trust, someone who will give you honest feedback, to help you rehearse the conversation. It will help you to prepare, to be clear, and to be less shaky in the moment.

It may help you to write out your comments beforehand. Script exactly what you want to go over, and at least have a list to refer to. There is nothing wrong with referring to the list if you need it. Most people do not need this, but I have met many who find it helpful to at least know that if they get flustered in a very difficult scenario, they will have their cheat sheet. In the conversation, they say something like, "I have a list here of the things I wanted to make sure we covered." There is nothing weird about that.

GET THE TONE RIGHT

The importance of getting the tone right in a conversation like this cannot be overestimated. It is crucial that your tone be one that displays care and respect for the person. Because of the way the brain works, the other person's emotional reactions will be greatly affected by the tone of your voice in your communication. If your tone is soft and caring, fewer fight-or-flight reactions get triggered in the other person, and more rational responses are likely to be evoked. If you are not angry, harsh, or shaming, the other person will be able to receive your message better. So monitor your tone as you speak. You will be glad you did, and it will be better for him or her.

Closely akin to tone is your perceived emotional presence. The other person will unconsciously feel supported and "held" through a difficult ending if he senses that you are really "there" with him. Empathize with him and validate how it must feel for him. If you do, he will have a better chance of taking that care with him and a greater likelihood of hearing the constructive aspects of what you are telling him. Remember that there is probably a lot that you have to say that could prove helpful if he can hear it, and your emotional presence will help that to occur.

VALIDATE THE PERSON AND THE RELATIONSHIP

Let the other person know that you care about her and your relationship. Say it clearly. "I hope you know how much I value you and our relationship, and I hope this won't come between us forever. That's important to me." Just let her know that you care about her and that the issues at hand are the reasons for the ending, not her as a person.

Likewise, be clear about the issue itself. Stay on message about why you are doing this, and stay objective about why the ending has to occur. That way, both of you will have a greater chance of keeping the issues and the person separate.

GET AGREEMENT

In a difficult conversation or ending, emotions are often felt strongly by the person on the receiving end. As a result, what just happened might get fuzzy or even lost. So, at the end of the conversation, get agreement on what has happened and what is to follow, if any further steps are required.

"What have you heard me say?" is a good clarifying way to do this. "I want to make sure that we are going away with a good understanding of each other." If he comes back with a distortion, you can clarify at that point. "No, I am not saying that you are bad in some way. I am just saying that I need to make this change for the reasons I have said. I hope you can hear it that way and not as an attack on you. Are you clear on that?"

There are a lot of different ways to do this, and helping the person correct his distortions can benefit him and also prevent a misinterpretation of what was said.

Leave the conversation with hope and encouragement as well. "I hope that you can do well in the future and that you can take this experience in a way that will help you and not hurt you. That is my wish for you."

DEAL WITH DEFENSIVENESS AND REACTIONS

If you are dealing with a difficult person who gets defensive or argumentative, do not let that get you off message. The best formula I know for this is a combination of empathy and returning to the issue: "I understand that this is frustrating to you and that it is hard to hear. But I want you to understand what I am saying here, and need to make myself perfectly clear. This really is an issue, and it is not going away, and I need you to hear that."

Many times, as we saw in the section on fools in chapter 7, the person will not like hearing what you are saying and may not even get it. But the only person you can control in the conversation is yourself, so stay on message. Whether or not she gets it is not in your control. But remaining empathetic and clear *is* in your control. She cannot take that away from you unless you let her. So don't let that happen. Hold on to your power, the power of self-control.

YOU MAY NEED OTHERS

Sometimes there is so much danger of distortion by some personalities that you should make sure that you have someone in the conversation with you—especially if there is danger of litigation or other bad outcomes. A good HR person, a friend, an attorney, or another manager can all be good backup, depending on the situation or context. Do not feel that that is overkill, as sometimes to not have it is underkill. You may need that witness if you end up in court or even to help handle the conversation itself. "Don't take a knife to a gunfight" is good advice. In extreme cases, you might want your attorney to have the conversation for you, especially if evil is present in the situation.

Related to this is the need for good notes and immediate documentation of what occurred. Many times when someone comes after you later, he will be fuzzy with the facts. The better the documentation you have, especially of the path that led to the ending, the better off you will be. Judges and juries will be impressed with the one who has a clear, provable record of the facts. Again, consult your legal help if you are in a situation that is in this league.

OFTEN, THE OUTCOME IS GOOD

My friend was stuck in her dating life, and it was time to do one right. She was ready to end another short-term dating relationship by just disappearing and dropping out of sight, off of his radar. I told her that if she ever wanted to get where she wanted to be in life and in dating, she had to learn to be more forthright about endings and delivering bad news to people. And I told her that if she wanted my help anymore, she had to call this guy and tell him that she had enjoyed going out with him but that she did not see a future with him and wanted to let him know that she did not want to go out anymore.

She resisted, but she finally made the call. When she did, she was jolted. Expecting the worst, she got the opposite. He said, "I just want to thank you for telling me this in a straightforward manner. You have restored my faith in women and also saved me a lot of time and effort by not continuing to go out with me if it were not going to go anywhere. I wish all women would do what you just did."

She could not believe it, but I just gave her a "told you so" coach's nod. It not only helped him, but it also took her to a whole new level of functioning in her relationships with men. Not long after that, she finally attracted the kind of guy she had been looking for: honest, responsible, and kind. Why? She had to become that sort of person first before she was going to attract one. That is one of the reasons I had her make that call in the first place. It was not just for him, but also for her development. She had to become what she was looking for before she would ever find it.

You will find the same thing. The clearer and kinder you are in your communication of endings and bad news to people, the better the people you will find yourself surrounded by in life and work. You attract what you are. So do this for them but also for you. You'll be glad you did.

EXCEPT IN RARE CASES, DON'T BURN BRIDGES

With evil people, as I have said, burn the bridge. But with everyone else, make the ending one that leaves an impression and a real understanding that you are someone who is kind, honest, and respectful. Even though in this situation things did not work out, you never know when you might cross paths with that person again. Next time, it may be in a deal that will work, or he may be a different person a few years from now. If you leave things in good shape, you will be able to pick up where you left off, in a good place, and have a good outcome next time if the situation or opportunity is right. You always win by treating people well. "Do unto others as you would have them do unto you" is good not only for them but for you, as well. You never know when you will see them again or when life or business may take an unexpected turn and bring you back together.

Who knows? The person you've just ended something with may be your boss or lender or investor one day. Make sure you do this well!

ABOVE ALL, DON'T BE SQUISHY

Remember, at this point, you have decided on an ending. So end it and leave it clearly over. Many times people leave a little wiggle room or false hope just to soften the bad news. Do not do that if an ending is what you desire. Otherwise, you are just going to have to do it again. If it is over, make sure that at the end of the conversation, it is over. Don't leave an open door or window if you don't want one. Close it now, so you will not have to do it again.

CHAPTER 12

Embrace the Grief:
The Importance of Metabolizing
Necessary Endings

M oe Girkins, a former AT&T executive, is the CEO of Zondervan Publishers, a division of HarperCollins (my publisher). When I told her I was writing a book on necessary endings and how difficult but important they are, she told me a story.

"I know exactly what you mean," she said. "I saw this at AT&T when I was there. I had to oversee the closing of a company we owned. It had been there for decades, and the people had invested their lives there. When we had to shut it down, I knew we had to do it right."

"So what did you do?" I asked.

"Well, I had a funeral," she said.

"A funeral?" I asked.

"Yes, exactly," she said. "A real ceremony to say good-bye."

"What did that look like?"

"Well, we got everyone together and told stories, reminisced, and cried. We celebrated the past and said good-bye to it. And we buried a time capsule."

"A time capsule?"

"Yes. We asked everyone to put something in the time capsule and told them that we would bury it on the site. The building was going away, and we wanted them to feel that although the business was ending, we would celebrate what they had all done over the years and preserve it for the future. It was really healthy, and it allowed them to say good-bye, leave it behind, and move on to the next stage.

"I knew that they had had so much invested in it that if we did not allow them to have a proper good-bye, they would not be able to move on. People can't really disinvest themselves and move on unless they say good-bye to what has been. They need that sense of closure. And once they had that, it was amazing how they were able to go through the transition. But without it, I don't think it would have happened as well. It was very important."

Smart move, I thought. Pretty good for a nonpsychologist, and certainly a sign of a good leader. Why? The reason is basic physics. If you have emotional and other energy invested in something, when you pull that out, and let go, you are going to feel it. For every action there is an equal and opposite reaction, so if you make a move to end something you are invested in, there will be an impact. And if you do not deal with those feelings, you are going to have to do some funny things to get around them.

So why does that matter?

Pure and simple: *energy and investment*. Whatever you are going to build in your life or your business, it is going to come through investment of energy by you and your people in the new *fill-in-the-blank*. And the only energy you can invest is available energy. To make it available, you have to withdraw it from something else. The technical word for that in psychology is to decathect. *Cathexis* is the investment of mental or emotional energy in a person, an object, or an idea. So *decathexis* is the process of taking it back. The only way to do that is to grieve for what has been invested in before so you can move forward.

The grieving process is a mental and emotional letting go. What that means is to face the reality that it is over, whatever *it* is, and to feel the feelings involved in facing that reality. It means to come out of the denial and numbness emotionally and feel whatever you feel. The reason that helps, though, is that grief has movement to it. It goes somewhere. It goes forward. Feeling the anger helps get the protest out of the way, and feeling the sadness helps move the letting go further along. It gets people unstuck. When people do not feel their feelings, positive and negative, about something significant that has ended, they will remain tethered to it in some way.

That is why the feelings involved in grief are unique. Unlike emotions that do not take us anywhere and in fact can keep us stuck, the feelings of grief have *forward motion* to them. When you feel grief, you are saying, "I am looking this reality right in the face and dealing with it, the reality that this [whatever *this* is] is *over. Finished.* Grief also means I am getting ready for what is next, because I am finishing what is over."

The danger when people do not face their grief is twofold. First, to keep from facing it, they sometimes continue to beat a dead horse, hanging on to false hope or staying angry at what is past. They get stuck in protesting reality. Second, denying the grief often leads people to do strange things on the rebound, which are really attempts to keep from feeling the grief involved in letting go. It is a defense mechanism.

I once was in a consulting session with an executive team whose members were confused as they were charting their future. They were particularly troubled by the rabbit trails they felt their CEO had taken them down several times.

"What were those?" I asked. They said that he had come up with these "big visions" a few times and steered the billion-dollar enterprise in a direction that got them off mission and diverted a lot of resources that they really needed.

"There was _____ project," they said. "And then there was the whole _____ debacle. And after that, there was the _____ strategy."

Each one had been a disaster and had taken a lot of money, time, and people. Then I had a thought.

"When were these, and what else was going on?" I asked.

"What do you mean?" they asked me back.

I elaborated. "What years did these happen in and what was going on in between, before, and after?"

What we found was amazing. On the big whiteboard in the boardroom, I constructed a chart that was more than revealing. We did a timeline over fifteen years, and an astounding pattern emerged. Each time something did not go well that the CEO was really emotionally invested in, *immediately thereafter he would launch one of the initiatives that had been a big problem.* In other words, to deal with a downturn in normal operations, disappointing results, or failure, instead of dealing with that loss and the grief involved in it, the CEO would grasp a "rebound relationship" with a new vision. It is the business version of the person who loses a lover, and instead of processing the grief, immediately jumps into a rebound relationship. You have seen how that works out, usually not good.

The reason is that the new whatever is chosen out of need, not merit. The person rushes to something new to avoid feeling the grief, disappointment, and loss. He idealizes the new but seldom thinks about the long term in those instances. He is just thinking, *What can I do that feels better than I feel right now?*

The discussion led to some important coaching with the executive team as to how to identify this tendency in their leader and how to work with it when it emerged. It also underscored to them, as it should to us, the necessity of "metabolizing" our losses, including endings. The truth is that to the degree we were invested in something that's ending, we will have to work the grief through our system in order to be ready for whatever is next. In this instance, to avoid that working-through process, the CEO was just getting active for no truly good reason.

So, just like Moe Girkins, treat the endings with respect. Memorialize them, if appropriate. Whatever it takes to get the needed closure, do it. These symbols can help to make an ending easier. When someone dies, we have a ceremony, a funeral, to say good-bye. We even at times all put a bit of dirt on the grave, or toss some of the ashes into the ocean. The act symbolizes so much to us: the love we shared with someone, the value that we had for them and they for us, the celebration of a life well lived, and the psychic space to satisfy our very real need to feel our sorrow. Symbols and symbolic events do a lot to help us get our mind around an ending.

The good-bye party, the good-bye lunch to launch someone into their next season, or on the negative side of the equation, even the burning of the divorce papers—all play a part in helping the two sides of the brain to embrace and process what has actually happened. In significant endings, you must face your grief, and sometimes symbols help to do that.

METABOLIZE THE ENDING TO YOUR BENEFIT

Joe was leaving a company that he had started five years before. Initially, the business had gone very well. It was bought out by a private equity group, which left him in place as the CEO. But slowly the relationship between him and the investors hit the skids, and after another year, the investors began to wind down his role and move him out. It was a lot of pain for both sides, but fortunately his position as founder was strong enough to help him get out in a good position, at least financially. Because of that, he felt pretty successful.

With his sails somewhat full of wind, he hit the streets looking for backers for his next deal. He was ready to go. But when we met, I had a different perspective.

"Joe, I don't think you are ready for your next deal, at least not yet," I said.

"Why not?" He pushed back. "I think you have to go when the momentum is there, and with this payout following the purchase, I think the buzz is pretty good right now."

"That is the problem," I said. "You probably *could* get a deal. And you would make all the same mistakes you made in the last one, and I don't want you to do that. We need to do an autopsy."

"An autopsy?"

"Yep. That is where you dissect the body to see what killed it, and we need to do that with you," I told him.

The conversation got really interesting after that, as he had never really thought that there was much to be harvested from past experience, especially ones that didn't go well. He was a "shake it off and move on" kind of guy. So when I said that I wanted to look at all aspects of the last deal, especially the parts that did not go well, he was surprised. But in my view, that is exactly why he had some long-standing patterns that had never really been overcome and seemed to still get in the way of his enormous gifts in a lot of what he did. So we got to work on "metabolizing" his ending.

What does that look like? Think of what you do when you metabolize food: You take it in (ingest it), and your body breaks the food down and recognizes its components as falling into two big groups. The first group is what is usable to you, the vitamins, minerals, and other nutrients. It takes all of the good stuff and turns it into things that you can use: fuel and structure. It keeps you going, and it literally becomes part of you. Want bones? Eat calcium. You get the picture.

The second group, the parts of food that are not usable, is called waste. And what do we do with waste? We eliminate it and get it out of the system. In fact, if you can't eliminate waste, you get sicker as the days go on. So your body takes what it ingests, uses what is usable, takes that forward, and eliminates what it can't use, leaving that behind.

In love and in work, experience is the "food" of life. Just as "You are what you eat," you are what you experience as a person. You "ingest" experience like food, taking it in, and it becomes part of you. To metabolize experience, whether in significant relationships or in business, you have to do what your body does with food: *keep what is usable to you, and eliminate what is not.*

You have to look at the experience and break it apart. What was good about it? The relationships? The learnings? The new skills you attained? The modeling you saw? New knowledge? Your strengths? Take all of that and consciously make it a part of you, savor it, remember it, cement it, build on it, focus on it so it is not lost. It will become new "cells and bones," parts of you that we refer to as wisdom, experience, or character. You will take it with you and be stronger and wiser for it if you heed the learning that was in that experience.

And on the negative side, there are some items that you will want to eliminate. You saw some things, did some things, had some things done to you, and perhaps you have some shrapnel from the battle that you need to dig out. Some splinters in your feet. Maybe you also shot some people yourself, and some amends are in order. Maybe you made other mistakes or saw some weaknesses you didn't know you had. Whatever happened that was negative, take the wisdom out of it, learn from it, and then eliminate what is not useful to you. The pain, the bitterness, the feelings of failure, the loss and grief, and the resentment all need to be eliminated and left behind. But left behind *consciously*, as opposed to just denied and forgotten.

How? Different people eliminate crummy feelings in different ways, but in general you need to talk them out, cry if you have to, feel your feelings, express them, forgive, and let it all go. Leave it behind after you have given it adequate attention. Decathect. If you do that, then you will be ready for whatever is next, having learned and benefited from what you have gone through, positive or negative, and you will show up in your next deal or relationship fully ready, *even readier than you would have been had you not gone through it*. No matter what happened, you are the better for it.

But if you don't metabolize the last one, you are probably, like Joe, going to repeat the mistakes and not benefit from what you could have learned. You will have the same blind spots that lead you to trust the wrong person or be impulsive without due diligence or underestimate your strengths and real value again, thereby selling yourself short one more time and leaving money on the table. Whatever you did should be reflected upon and metabolized in the way we have described. Even in the deals that went well—you should know why, so you can capitalize more and more on whatever made that happen.

TEAM METABOLIZING

I recently led an executive team retreat in which the focus was metabolizing the last big venture that the company had done. We spent a lot of time breaking down the experience and finding what was useful and what needed to be eliminated. There were mistakes discovered that led to structural changes in the company so that they would not happen again. There were lessons learned from the partners that the team was able to capture and institutionalize into some of their own processes. There were some personnel decisions that they were forced to make.

One geographical shift also was seen as necessary to keep the mistakes from ever occurring again. They moved some operations. There were team dynamics and working patterns that, once examined, they all committed to changing. On the positive side of that, when they looked at the contributions that each had made, they found a strength in one of the team members that they did not know she had and figured out ways to capitalize on that in the future. They changed her total focus. And as we went through the entire process, a huge strategic shift emerged as a result of looking at all the pieces. *They left knowing more about their future from examining the last big deal than they would have if they had gone on a planning retreat.* It was huge. But the lesson is that we should be doing this all the time as a matter of course, and pruning the bush.

PERSONAL ENDINGS

"Stop it!" I said to Jennifer. "Don't even think about it!"

"Why? I think it will be great for me," she said.

"Not a chance," I replied. "The *last* thing you need to do right now is to be dating. That is like an alcoholic getting a job as a bartender or event planner. It is the worst idea ever."

What we were discussing was Jennifer's immediate signing up with a dating service right after her divorce. In fact, I don't even think the divorce was final yet, and she was already getting ready to get back out there, thinking, "I will find a good one this time."

Fat chance, I knew. She had several patterns in the ways she related to men that were going to ensure another bad choice and another failure. She had done it twice, gravitating to the alpha male who made her feel secure, and later finding that the relationship held no space for her, her opinions, or her needs. It "always had to be his way," she said. Surprise? Look up *alpha male*. But that was her "type," as she put it.

There were other dynamics too, both in her selection process and in the ways that she related to a man once she was dating him, that did not bode well. Bright and attractive and very much fun to be around, she had never had difficulties finding men. But the ones she would find, and what she would let them get away with or enable them to do—that was a different story, and exactly why I did not want her out there until she did some metabolizing.

So I talked her into enrolling in a divorce recovery class for six months before she began dating again. In that process, she made some huge discoveries. One day, she said, "I am learning that I have some issues with men." *Really? Wow! How about that?* I thought.

"Gosh, Jennifer, that's great. I am glad that the class is helping you," I said.

"It is the best thing I ever did. I am going to be so much better in the choices I make when I get out there dating again. But I am nowhere near being ready. I think I need to take some time for myself, make sure I have worked through Jason, and not go on some rebound and make the same mistake again," she said. "What do you think?"

"I think that sounds like a plan," I said, biting back more than a few "I told you so's." Either way, I am glad that she did the metabolizing that she needed to do. It served her well, and about a year later, she found a good one as a result of the work she had done in relation to the last one. She took the lessons that were usable and eliminated from her life the pain that was not. So this time, she did not repeat it. Whew.

THE BOTTOM LINE

At any given moment, you are an amalgam of what has happened up until that moment. So if your last experience has been properly metabolized, you are ready. You have learned, made the changes necessary, added whatever you need, and are wiser and more prepared. Facing your grief, working it through, and letting it equip you is a significant part of a good necessary ending.

Two questions to consider as you reflect on your next necessary ending:

- What situation are you ending, or going to end, about which you should do some "metabolizing" work?
- What project, strategy, loss, or other initiative should you and your team spend some "metabolizing" time on?

CHAPTER 13

Sustainability: Taking Inventory of What Is Depleting Your Resources

Webster defines *sustainable* as referring to "a method of harvesting or using a resource so that the resource is not depleted or permanently damaged." When I looked it up, I expected the definition to include something like the ability to "keep something going." But Webster says it much better with a focus on the depletion or damaging of the resource itself.

The lesson: if you are doing something that is using you or your resources in a way that is depleting you or damaging you, you can't keep it going. The reason? You are not just getting tired; you or your resource is getting *depleted*. You or your resource is being cannibalized. In short: you will run out. That adds so much to the discussion.

What does this look like in real life? It is what we see when people do not do the necessary endings that their hearts, minds, souls, bodies, and bank balances are telling them over and over that they need to do. As a result, something gets depleted:

- A CEO or boss drives his people toward a strategy that stretches them past their abilities to keep going, so they get depleted and lose heart.
- A business owner pushes herself day and night to get her startup going and begins to get sick more and more.
- A CEO or manager allows a toxic employee to make the culture negative for others, to the point where the entire staff becomes demotivated as time goes on.
- A spouse tries over and over to be accepting and forgiving of an angry or disrespectful mate, and begins to lose heart for the person, the relationship, and for love itself.
- A business initiative has a great start, but costs are greater than planned, and the cash burn grows faster and hotter.
- A business keeps hoping for a profit, and takes on more and more debt, always thinking that the turnaround is coming, even as debt grows.
- In between jobs or with reduced income, an individual or a family continues to live at the same standard of living they had when income was flush.
- A person finds himself totally miscast, in a job, career, or position that has nothing to do with his talents, strengths, or passions.

Think of the results of all of those scenarios, and you will see how profound sustainability really is. In each one, as time goes on, something or someone is getting *depleted* or *damaged*. For that reason, sustainability is one of the most important reasons for a necessary ending. If you are doing anything that by definition cannot continue because the source itself is being depleted or damaged, an ending is not only necessary, it is vital and urgent.

In my experience with businesses and individuals, not paying attention to sustainability is one of the most common reasons that they get into trouble, sometimes unrecoverable trouble. Why? Because the assets, be they financial or human, get totally spent. At that point, the people or businesses are out of options, and no good choices remain. Sustainability keeps options alive, and as long as you have options, you have hope. But without the ability to keep going because you or your other assets are gone, you have very limited choices and are forced to accept options that you would not have chosen. Therefore, there are few better contexts to execute endings than in situations that are unsustainable.

What I want you to take away from this discussion is the push to look at some areas of your life and work that may be on an unsustainable path. So let's look at some questions that might help you honestly assess your situation:

- Are you in an emotional state right now that is not sustainable? I am not talking about just a "hard time" or a time that you would not *want* to continue forever. Life is full of difficulties, but with proper support and other resources, we can endure them if we have to and if we have a good reason to. What I am referring to is a hard time that is truly not sustainable and often continues for no good reason. Are you in a state that is eating your heart, mind, soul, or energy in such a way that you are headed for some sort of crash or burnout?
- Are you in a physical state right now that is not sustainable? Too much travel? Too little sleep? Too much "on the go"? Too much taxing of your physical system? For a prolonged period of time with no end in sight? Too little exercise? Too much junk food?
- Are you in a state right now in your relationships that is not sustainable? Is there some relationship that is depleting or damaging you? Is there a context in which you

feel compromised or forced to adapt to another person's needs and demands out of fear? Are you in a situation where someone has power over you and is slowly diminishing you?

- Are you in a professional state right now that is not sustainable? In your work, is something going on in the culture or in your relationship with your boss that you cannot continue long-term without some sort of damage to your drive, talents, or passion? This does not include all difficult cultures or bosses, as most people have some period of time in a setting like that, which really builds them or equips them over time, even if it is hard. What I am referring to is something that is not equipping you or causing you to grow but is slowly wearing you down or killing something inside of you.

- Are you in a spiritual state right now that is not sustainable? In your spirit, is something causing you to be diminished? Is hope being deferred in some way that is causing a sickness of spirit? Are you losing a sense of meaning in life? Is something happening that is causing you to feel depleted of a sense of purpose, mission, transcendence, love, or other spiritual dimensions? A diminished belief in humanity or diminished faith? Is your ability to hope being affected?

- Are you in a financial state right now that is not sustainable? In your business or personal finances, are your expenses greater than what's coming in, with no end in sight? Is the curve between investment and certain returns way out of whack? Do you not know how your real, fixed, non-negotiable expenses are going to be covered in the current path that you are on? Said another way, if something does not change, are you going to run out of money and have no options? If "cash equals options," are you on a path of diminishing options?

- Are your energy reserves being depleted in a way that is not sustainable? Is there something so draining to your energy that you have to make yourself keep going? Do you have to drag yourself in a particular path continually? Is there a clear drain that is causing that?

- Are you letting your strengths fall into disuse in a way that is not sustainable? Are you on a course where your strengths are not available to you? Are you being cornered, at work or elsewhere, in a way that requires you to be "not you" most of the time? Is the real you slowly going to sleep? Do you fear that it may not be able to be reawakened?

- Do you find yourself in a situation where you are over-extended in some way, one that began as an anomaly but now has become a pattern? Many times this happens with a person's schedule or workload. What they thought was going to be a lot of work or extra hours or effort for a while has now become what is required to keep it all going, as the entity or enterprise has become *shaped and formed around exactly that ingredient, all that effort from just one source—you.* So what was supposed to be a season has now become a pattern, the new normal.

All of these scenarios are examples in which continuing to spend yourself or other resources diminishes or does damage to you or them. That is not sustainable long-term, which means that you are on a path to an end of something, a part of either you or your business, and not by choice. And that is a fact that you cannot ignore.

Remember that I am not talking about sacrifice or other kinds of proactive decisions that a person makes to go forward in something that costs them. We all do that, and it is an important requirement for maturity. We choose difficult paths for good reasons. What I am talking about is a passive and negative state that you find yourself in over time, a state with no benefits and nothing but diminishing returns. That is not sustainable.

So remember to watch out for those situations in life or in business that diminish you or your assets over time. That should be an alarm to move immediately to stop the outflow, reorganize, bring in some sort of help, make a change, or do some kind of ending, which is more than necessary. It is vital in the truest sense of the word. It does not mean that you have to end anything in the "big picture," but it does mean that you have to end at least the dynamic that is unsustainable. For example, I talked earlier about a spouse in an unsustainable position with an addict husband. She did not end her marriage, but she did end the dynamic that was destroying her and their relationship, one that was unsustainable.

So take inventory, and look at what is net negative in any of the life categories. If it is not leading somewhere that will end up reversing the negative outflow, plan an ending. I suggest also that you ask yourself where you are in the timeline of sustainability. Just as a business has to know its cash position and when it will run out, you have to know that in all of the above dimensions as well. Try this: ask yourself whether you are in the first, second, or third trimester of when you are going to run out and be fully depleted. Let that be a guide to exactly how urgent *urgent* has to be. Then get moving. Everything depends on it.

CHAPTER 14

Conclusion: It's All About the Future

My friend Brian and I were having dinner a few months ago, right in the middle of the writing of this book. I could not help but focus in on the endings aspect of what he was saying. When I asked him how he was doing, he basically, without knowing it, practically repeated the entire book to me.

"I am in a great place," he said. "I never in my wildest dreams would have thought that I would have ended up where I am now, but I am just very grateful."

"What in particular were you thinking about?" I asked.

"Well, I just went on this silent retreat, and part of the emphasis was to meditate on gratitude. I was instructed to think, mull over, meditate on, and savor all of the things that I could think of that I was grateful for. And I realized something," he said.

"What was that?" I asked him.

"I realized that so much of my life, the really good stuff, came about not really at all as a result of my being smart enough to plan it that way. In fact, it even made me more grateful to see that. I could never have planned my life the way that it has unfolded. It has been a total gift, I believe."

"What led you to the insight that it was better than you had planned?" I inquired.

"Well, I looked at the whole picture. I know this sounds a little too idealistic, but it is true. I am in a place now in midlife where I absolutely love my work, each and every day. I am financially set for life, even if I never work another day. I am in a really good marriage with really great kids. I have wonderful friends and community. I could go on and on. Not that it is perfect by any measure. You know the traumas that I have gone through," he said. "But the big picture of it all is that it is healthy. It has life to it. I am surrounded by good people and by meaningful activities."

"Yeah, that is true," I said. "You have a pretty good picture in its entirety."

"But what I realized was that all of it—from my wife to what I do to the community of friends that I have, the whole thing—was not something I really knew how to do. It all came from something else," he said.

"Something else?" I asked.

"Yes. None of it was what I put on a whiteboard at twenty-five and said, 'I want that woman, that job, that neighborhood, et cetera.' All of it came from whatever I did *before*. Then, when the 'before' ended, it led to the 'next thing.' I could not have ever planned all of the 'next steps.' But there was a pattern that emerged. Every time something ended, that ending led to the next thing that was what I needed and was looking for," he said.

When I heard him say *ending*, I asked him to say more. Authors do that when they are writing a book on a certain topic and there is an illustration of it standing right there. Little did I know how true that was, until he kept going.

"Well, I don't know how to describe it all, but I realized that it always took some kind of ending of one thing to get to the next. Out of that step, whatever it was, the next level was born. When I left my old company and joined the next one, if you remember, it just opened everything all up. It took it to a huge new level that I could not have foreseen. My job, it seems, was just to take the step that seemed right, and take the step of ending one thing so the next could happen. When I did, it always came.

"Remember the woman that I dated before Jil? Many people thought she was 'the one.' But I knew that there were some things that were important to me that were missing. Again, it took a big step to end that relationship, but that is when Jil came along.

"Then, after the company grew, all of those new and bigger opportunities came along because I saw that Jeremy and I were great friends and had been great business partners in those growth years but weren't really going in the same direction. So we had to split. I had to end our partnership. And when that ending came, look what emerged! That is when all of this came along, and the rest is history. But I could never have foreseen any of that. That is what makes me grateful. Every time, the next step 'just came.' It just did.

"But . . . I have to say something. In this retreat, I also had to be a little proud of myself, kind of grateful to me, if you will. Not in terms of making great things happen, because I see all of the good stuff I have, as I have said, as a gift from above. One thing led to the next, and I did not or could not have planned it. But what I am proud of is that each time it was time to take the step, I did have the courage, and the trust and faith, to end what I needed to end in order for the next thing to happen.

"As I am talking to my son about success, that is the picture that is coming together for me. I am telling him, Son, let me give you the formula. First, you have to do the very, very best you can do at each step along the way. Wherever you find yourself, be the best you can be and make the best out of whatever that is. Make it work the best that it can work, doing whatever is in your power.

"Second, when it is time to have the courage to take the next step, you have to do that and not be afraid. I am not talking about being risky or making stupid moves. But I am talking about not being afraid to take bold steps when it is obviously time. That takes courage and faith, but you have to do that when it is time.

"Then, third, return to the first thing I said. Pour yourself into where you find yourself and make it all that it can be. And if it was a wrong step, that won't matter, because you would have performed well, learned some things in the process, and people will notice your performance and will value it. That is why you won't have to worry about tomorrow, because you will have done so well yourself, even if it is a bad deal or outcome. People will know from watching you. And you will be ready for what is next.

"So, I just had this incredible awareness that in a strange way, everything I have that is of value has come from being willing to end something that I was doing and go to the next step. The endings and the great new beginnings are somehow linked together. You can't have one without the other. It is a weird paradox, but that is what I really think."

I could not improve on that. It illustrates so well what we have been talking about throughout this book. Your next step always depends on two ingredients: how well you are maximizing where you are right now and how ready you are to do what is necessary to get to the next place. And sometimes that depends on ending some of what is happening today. As my friend's path illustrates, that is a winning combination for the best tomorrow you can find. You do your part, have faith, and tomorrow will take care of itself. But remember, for the right tomorrow to come, some parts of today may have to come to a necessary ending.

Acknowledgments

Every book has its own life, and this one was no exception. It began in the day-to-day trenches and war rooms of many excellent leaders, in various businesses, over many years, as they grappled with dilemmas involving difficult, but necessary, endings. From there, the patterns began to be clear and the next step was to somehow figure out how to communicate both the necessity, and the difficulty, of those crucial endings in one book. It happened with the help of a few people whom I would like to thank.

Hollis Heimbouch, my publisher at Harper, was instrumental in helping me integrate the tandem themes of how endings affect not only business, but life. Her big picture acumen, along with the line-by-line help, added much to keeping the business and the personal tethered, as they are in real life. Her ability to walk in many pairs of shoes was clear throughout.

Jan Miller and Shannon Marven, my literary agents—to you I cannot say enough thanks. Jan, for your scope of publishing knowledge and strategic input that gives feet to many missions—thanks for helping me with mine. And Shannon, you are a rock star. Unsurpassed in the hard work of making publishing projects work in the right place at the right time in the right way.

To Sandy Vander Zicht for her editorial help as well. As usual, I find a way to use more words than are necessary and you "ended" that tendency well in many instances. :-)

Matt Inman at Harper, thanks for all of your hard work keeping it all moving forward and for the technical expertise needed for those hard questions.

Index

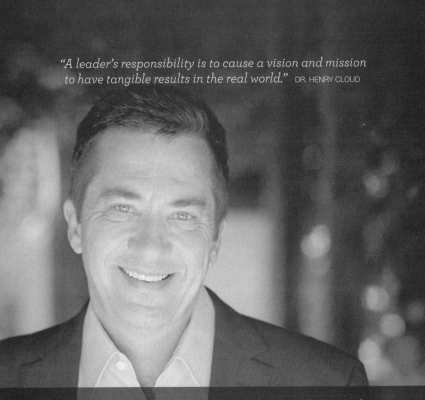